The
Art
of
Biography

By Paul Murray Kendall

RICHARD THE THIRD
WARWICK THE KINGMAKER
THE YORKIST AGE

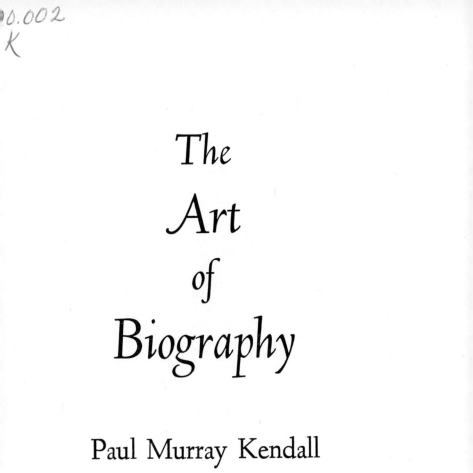

The
Art
of
Biography

Paul Murray Kendall

W · W · NORTON & COMPANY, INC ·

NEW YORK

TO
SIGGY, KATE, and SILKY
with love

Contents

Introduction

ONLY TO KEEP the memory of so worthy a friend and fellow, alive . . ." Thus Shakespeare's actor-colleagues, Heminges and Condell, justified their labors in preparing a collected edition of his plays, the First Folio of 1623.

Writers of biography envy, though they cannot afford to be guided by, such a purpose; for the biographer's mission is to perpetuate a man as he was in the days he lived—a spring task of bringing to life again, constantly threatened by unseasonable freezes.

What a man leaves behind him after he dies is a mess of paper: birth certificate, school grades, diary, letters, check stubs, laundry lists . . . This paper trail, extending from his entrance to his exit, is what the biographer tries to tread—after he has sorted it out, that is.

If the man is long dead, scanty documents will be patched out by doubtful chronicles, perhaps legends; if he is recently dead, and sufficiently famous, there will be piled on the masses of his own paper, including perhaps transcribed telephone conversations, the mountainous recollections of friends and enemies, newspaper clippings, magazine "exposés."

A mess of paper: this is the promised land, or the prison, of the biographer.

That military genius, Clausewitz, once observed that strategy and tactics are essentially simple but that, in war, even the simplest thing is difficult. The objects and the means of biography are simultaneously obvious and obscure. On the trail of another man, the biographer must put up with finding himself at every turn: any biography uneasily shelters an autobiography within it. He begins with somebody else's papers, and ends with his own; and what goes on between, spread over years, is an unholy jumble of digging for facts, trying to understand what is found, and struggling to convey that understanding by literary effects which will transmute information into a life being lived, without betraying either the subject or the author.

With luck, the book which the biographer finally produces, in a decade or so, may be welcomed, with moderate warmth, by the world. How he went about it, the devils at which he hurled his inkwell, even the kind of literary organism he has created—such considerations seem hardly to matter. The workshop of the life-writer attracts few visitors.

Biography tends to be regarded as a rather mechanical process of arranging information so that it tells the story of a life, a sort of assembly-line that puts facts together. The practitioner of life-writing, on the other hand, sees in that image none of the lineaments of his trade. In a moment of candor he will tell you, with a simplicity honed by frustration, that biography is the craft-science-art of the impossible.

He will cheerfully acknowledge the view of the life-writer as a rather grubby creature, hived in a library and sweating ink onto 3 x 5 cards as he scavenges from manuscripts and tomes the human detritus of the centuries; but, privately, he is likely to see himself as a creature of desperation, bound to an implausible and bizarre enterprise. All too readily he perceives the gulf between his words, however evocative, and the reality of the life itself—its obscure currents of passion, its overt motivations masking wild desires, its skin-deep sorrows and illusory hopes and unrecorded miseries, commingling with "the apple tree, the singing, and the gold."

Biography must always be a flawed achievement and the biographer, a man who fails before he begins. There is no Othello with whom to compare Shakespeare's Othello. There is no Trojan war with which to compare the *Iliad*. You cannot visit Satan in hell in order to learn how well Milton has taken him off. No one can accuse Thackeray of failing to tell all about Becky Sharp. But a biography is always publicly haunted by the life which it has attempted to recapture, and a biographer is always privately mocked by the evidences which that life has left behind. Unlike other writers, he must create a world out of materials which exist independently of what he does with them and of which he has had no part in the fashioning. No character that the novelist or the dramatist creates can be more intelligent, more complex, more sensitive, than his maker; whereas it is the lot of the biographer to pursue a man who is very likely to have been more ambitious, more subtle, more daring, and sharper of wits than he. In the race of art, a biographer must hoist himself by his bootstraps in order to run at all.

However, whether biography be labeled art or craft or science does not seem to worry biographers. Their mood is rather like that of Theodore Roosevelt when he said, "I took Panama and then let Congress debate about it afterward." Biography *is* a craft—like all the other arts—in that it employs techniques which can be learned by anybody, which are outside personal commitment. It can be loosely called a science in that, for part of his labors, the biographer proceeds inductively: he collects facts in order to arrive at conclusions from them. It is an art, however lowly, because the biographer is himself interfused into what he has made, and, like the novelist and the painter, shapes his material in order to create effects.

Yet there are far fewer great biographies than there are great novels and great poems and great dramas. The novelist's pen is a delicate instrument. If the biographer holds something like that pen in one hand, he has to wield a shovel with the other. His ore is not inner experience, the quicksilver stuff of gland and nerve. It is brute matter, wrested from the earth. The biographer must be a sort of bifurcated animal, digger and dreamer; for biography is an impossible amalgam: half rainbow, half stone. To exist at all, it must feed upon the truth of facts, and yet to exist on its highest level, it must pursue the truth of interpretation. In a way, biography means just what the Greek words that compose it mean—*bios*, life, and *graphein*, to write. Yet, though the art has been practiced with distinction for twenty-five hundred years, it was not, in the English-speaking world, until the seventeenth century that it achieved its name, not until the eighteenth that it secured something of a place of its own, and really not until the twentieth that it became firmly established.

A biographer who ventures to discuss the practice of life-writing can hardly do otherwise than work outward, as best he is able, from the nucleus of his own experience to the labors and achievements of biographers in general.

In my first chapter, "Walking the Boundaries," I have therefore sought to pluck biography, gingerly, from its context in time in order to view it floating free in space, as it were, to peer at it from above and below, touching here and prodding there, so as to get at identity by examining its dimensions, its elements, the pressure and tensions that give it shape.

In my next four chapters I have surveyed biography from its beginnings to the First World War, not to provide a capsule history—there are a few histories available—but rather to spy out the peculiarities and the patterns, the relations of biography with its milieu, which come to light when lifewriting is stretched along the axis of time. The final chapter is an attempt to picture the state of biography in our contemporary society.

This venture, then, is not a critique nor a history nor a manual of biography. I would like to think of it as a small and perhaps disorderly exploring party sent out to reconnoiter terrain which expert scouts and trackers, but too few of them, have already penetrated.

Since the expedition travels light, and casually, I will dispense with acknowledgment of indebtedness—to biographers, critics, librarians—which might exaggerate my claims to competence and embarrass their learning.

Portions of this book were first developed in a series of lectures given under the auspices of the English Department of Wayne State University. To the members of that department, particularly to the Chairman, Dr. Herbert Schueller, I owe a large debt of thanks, no less for the hospitality than for the opportunity.

There are few windows opening on the world of life-writing. The handful of books and articles I found most helpful I will list here, as an expression of my gratitude and for your information: Catherine Drinker Bowen, *Adventures of a Biographer;* James L. Clifford, ed., *Biography as an Art* (available in paperback); Leon Edel, *Literary Biography* (paperback); John A. Garraty, *The Nature of Biography;* André Maurois, *Aspects of Biography;* Harold Nicolson, *The Development of English Biography;* Iris Origo, "Biography, True and False," *Atlantic* (CCIII, Feb.); Roy Pascal, *Design and Truth in Autobiography;* Mark Schorer, "The Burdens of Biography," *Michigan Quarterly Review* (I, 4, 1962).

Ohio University,
1964

The
Art
of
Biography

I

Walking the Boundaries

CONSIDER HOW uneasily biography lies between historical writing and belles lettres, somewhat disdainfully claimed by both.

For centuries, history regarded biography as a sort of poor relation, a hanger-on. An eighteenth-century historian perfectly reproduces the atmosphere of condescension when he confesses that he had "several times deviated and descended from the dignity of an historian, and voluntarily fallen into the lower class of biographers, annalists, etc." History regarded biography as trivial or, in kinder moments, fragmentary. The historian surveys the great scene. He deals with church and state, with the mighty issues of war and peace, with the growth of constitutions and the fall of kingdoms. The biographer contents himself with a single individual and the slight thread of happenings that form his life.

In our own time this attitude has been, if not abolished, at least modified. Historians in increasing numbers—particularly since the Second World War—have themselves become biographers. Yet, fledgling historians in our graduate schools are not encouraged, I believe, to con biographies or study the methods of biographical research.

The distinguished American historian Dumas Malone, in an essay, "Biography and History," warns the biographer that "in his efforts to procure factual materials" he "must be as laborious and painstaking as any historian and he must be equally honest in interpreting them." Biography, then, if akin to history, had better wash its grubby hands before joining the company.

The essential nature of life-writing, however, becomes obscured if it is classed as a branch of history. Both explore the remains of yesterday and, as arts, interpret those remains; and there ends the similarity. Socrates and Cleopatra made their way in the world by their wits rather than by their beauty, but we should hardly class them as fellow-intellectuals. The historian frames a cosmos of happenings, in which men are included only as event-producers or event-suffers. The biographer explores the cosmos of a single being. History deals in generalizations about a time, the Middle Ages; about a group of people in time, the United States since 1865; about an institution, the Inns of Court in the fifteenth century. Biography deals in the particularities of one man's life.

The relations of biography with the art of literature have been almost as uneasy as those of biography with history. With this difference. Biography is a genuine province of literature—the notion is accepted by default rather than by debate—but a province which that kingdom has generally tended to ignore.

Our formal institutions of learning have paid scant attention to life-writing. In the United States the ubiquitous "survey courses" in English and American literature will yield a few pages of Pepys, a passage of Colley Cibber's autobiography, a little more from Johnson's *Lives of the Poets*, a prudently ample selection from Boswell's *Johnson*, something from Franklin's autobiography, a bit of John Stuart Mill and Cardinal Newman and Henry Adams, and—to balance the autobiographies—a chapter from Strachey's *Queen Victoria*. This, from *Widsith* to *Wasteland*, is about all.

American universities offer courses in "creative writing," nonfiction writing, even the writing of criticism; and graduate schools of English teach the mystique of the scholarly article. But universities do not offer courses in how to write biography, and few of them offer courses in the history and appreciation of biographical literature.

Until the twentieth century, scholars and critics found little to say about life-writing. In our own day biographical criticism has achieved notable stature, but it has been mostly written by a handful of biographers—Harold Nicolson, André Maurois, James Clifford, Leon Edel, Catherine Drinker Bowen, Mark Schorer, Iris Origo, and a few others. The massive annual bibliography of writings on English and American literature, which has been appearing in the Publications of the Modern Language Association (PMLA) since 1956, contains in its multi-thousands of listings over this period only four books (all noted in my introduction) and two considerable articles on biography. Historians of literature likewise take little interest in life-writing, as may be seen in two examples from Oxbridge. C. S. Lewis' much admired *English Literature in the Sixteenth Century* (Oxford) allows fewer than four pages to the three greatest biographical works of the age:

More's *History of Richard III*, which inaugurates modern English prose, Roper's *Life of More,* and Cavendish's *Life of Wolsey.* The second edition of *The Concise Cambridge History of English Literature* (1961) adds a chapter on "The Age of T. S. Eliot," which manages to mention political orators, writers on education, radio-television scripts, but has nothing to say about biographers—except to class Lytton Strachey as a caricaturist.

Perhaps scholars and critics feel, not that biography wants charm but that it wants challenge, that it does not need the services of an interpreter. Gourmets all, feeding on those "jellies soother than the creamy curd," which emerge from the kitchens of "imaginative literature," they can hardly be expected to burn with a hard gemlike flame if they are fired by mere meat and potatoes. Yet if we grant that a man's life is elusive, complex, subtly nuanced, it seems rather paradoxical to assume that the attempt to recapture that life is an enterprise too bald to repay investigation.

By and large, our best biographies present men of high action or men of letters. It is not hard to see why. The events in such men's lives—counting books, of course, as events—work like giant screens on which may be viewed the motions of personality. The cannons at Marengo hammer out, for that moment, Napoleon's character, as *Utopia,* more delicately, traces the psychic lineaments of Thomas More.

The greatest biography in the world unfolds the life of a man of letters; and literary figures have, in general, probably enjoyed a disproportionate amount of attention. For one thing, biographers, being writers of a kind, are attracted to writers, partly, no doubt, in order to seek their own features in a kindred face. Furthermore, men of letters are schooled, by temperament and talent, to examine themselves rather more assiduously than other beings do, and thus offer the biographer eloquent source-materials; and tend to project themselves by gesture as well as by pen, and thus provide the biographer with provocative role-playings against which he can stage his own perception of character.

On the other hand, the biographer of a man of letters runs special risks, the dangers lurking in the subject's words: there have probably been composed more disappointing lives of literary men than of any other kind of human being. In some cases, the works have been cavalierly ignored, or scanted; in others, they are too recklessly or crudely plundered as biographical evidences; in still others, they are mechanically shunted to one side and dealt with separately, as though the life and the "letters" did not penetrate each other.

The novels of the novelist, the poems of the poet, are significant events of a literary life, as the fighting of an election campaign, or a battle, are significant events of a life of action. Both are inextricably woven into the texture of living, and both harbor symbolic enactions of personality. But a poem-event is, paradoxically, more difficult to translate into biographical terms than an action-event. Whereas the poem is tantalizingly closer to the heart of self than such outward, limited manifestations of character as an election campaign, and appears to offer more direct expression of personality, it may well turn out to be a subtle concealment or a deliberately stylized projection or a privately visioned myth of that personality. Event speaks a psychological language not always

easy to understand but universal; poems and plays often whis-
per in a secret tongue—or light flares along a rocky coast to
lure biographers to destruction.

Whatever paper trail the biographer treads, he shares the
trials of other men of letters. The obvious difference between
biography and poetry-novel-drama is, if enormous, not quite
so enormous as appears. It will not do simply to say that
biography is made out of fact (whatever that is) and fiction is
made out of fancy (whatever *that* is). The writer of fiction,
out of the mating of his own experience and his imagination,
creates a world, to which he attempts to give the illusion of
reality. The biographer, out of the mating of an extrinsic
experience, imperfectly recorded, and his imagination, recreates a world, to which he attempts to give something of the
reality of illusion. We demand that a novel, however romantic
or "experimental," be in some way *true to life;* we demand of
biography that it be *true to a life.* There is a difference in
meaning between the phrases; they join, however, in signifying not "factual" but "authentic"—and authenticity lies not
only in what we are given but in what we are persuaded to
accept.

The biographer often finds himself in the grip of an extra-
rational, even compulsive choice, not unlike that which de-
scends on the novelist or poet. The biographer's subject, it
might be said, is a man whom he would have longed to create
if he had not existed. Like the novelist, he must be continually
asking questions about his materials and suspecting the form
into which they, too quickly, fall—hoping for the patience to
reject easy devices and plausible solutions and brilliant break-
throughs, so that he may trap those shy, belated birds, the best

answers. The failed biography and the failed novel frequently suffer from an identical ill: the authors have taken their materials for granted.

In his questioning, the biographer, cherishing the obligations of science and the hopes of art, teeters on a precarious perch. There are times when he must resist the enticements of art in order to be true to biographical art, must build with stone instead of rainbow. A literary device, however admirable in itself, which thrusts biographical materials outside the dimensions of life-writing, ruptures truth more seriously, because less obviously, than outright error. There are times when the biographer must query apparent facts, "scientific" evidence, in order to be true to biographical science; must build with rainbow instead of stone. Facts which mock his vision of character may turn out not to be facts or to be facts which do not say what they seem to say.

Since such struggles are hidden in the biographer's workshop, I shall offer brief illustrations out of my own experience, both drawn from a biography of that fifteenth-century political adventurer, Warwick the Kingmaker. His life spiraled to a culmination of violence and death in the battle of Barnet, which he fought against Edward IV on Easter Sunday of 1471. The contemporary accounts of the field are not numerous but offer more details than such reports usually do.

Seeking to make as much as I could out of this last scene, both exciting and revealing, I cast the chapter in the historical present tense in order to transport the reader into the thick of the action at Warwick's side. The chapter turned out bold and vivid, so I thought. But my wife firmly informed me that it would not do, it did not ring right. Grudgingly, I began asking myself questions, and soon received unpalatable answers.

In the first place, the historical present, a tricky device at best, gave an unmistakably fictional air to the scene. What was worse, it wrenched awry the style of the book. I do not mean simply the shift from past tense to present. In biographical writing, one of the tasks of style is to set the "viewing distance" between the reader and the life. The distance should reflect the kind of materials out of which the biography is created: the more intimate the evidence—letters, diary, reminiscences—the nearer the reader can be brought to the subject. Scantily documented Charlemagne and intimately observed Winston Churchill refuse to dwell in the same biographical house.

No portrait of Warwick survives, no collection of family letters, no view of him in undress. Hints of personality must be mined from chronicle and document; his character displays itself on the large screen of action. I had to reject the historical present because it violated the "middle distance" already established, pretending to bring the reader closer to Warwick than the material warranted. If it seems obvious that I should have thought of all this before writing the chapter, I can but heartily agree.

In the second instance, an apparently documented fact collided head-on with my conception of Warwick himself and of his friend Louis XI of France, the famous "spider King." English accounts state that Warwick was paid for two journeys to the Continent in the summer of 1464. However, though he and Louis XI had indeed arranged a rendezvous for that summer, there is no record, or even the faintest suggestion, that the two met; and Louis' movements at this time were closely reported by the Burgundian historian, Chastellain, and by a Milanese ambassador who was a confidant of the king. Historians therefore assumed that Warwick had hidden himself at Calais, perhaps at the bidding of his sovereign Edward IV, who had no love for Louis.

This assumption, in my view, was false alike to the character of Warwick, who regarded himself as the mentor rather than the minister of King Edward, and to the character of King Louis, who was far too nervously voluble to have concealed an interview with the man of all men he longed to ensnare in his web and far too well informed to remain in ignorance of Warwick's presence at Calais. One document, a very solid-seeming document, was forcing the two men to behave as if they had fallen into trauma and lost their identities. The truth of fact simply did not square with psychological truth, as I saw it. Since I could neither accept nor ignore the former, I could only desperately scrabble for evidences to undermine it.

Fortunately, I at last dug out a series of counter-facts which indicated that Warwick was besieging castles in northern England at the time he was supposedly crossing the Channel, that the diplomatic journeys ascribed to him were actually made by two of his adherents, whose presence at Louis' court was fully vouched for, and hence that the clerk of the royal accounts, paying Warwick for his men's expenses, had wrongly assumed that the Earl himself performed the service.

In this case, pigheaded refusal to let "art" bow to "science" enabled me—I hope—to reconcile fact and vision, stone and rainbow.

There is one respect, quite apart from the practice of literary art itself, in which biography differs from purely imaginative literature.

The relations between the public and poetry-novel-drama are frequently centered in the writer; whereas the relations between the public and biography are governed by subject matter. True, there are anthologies of poetry, drama, stories, arranged according to theme; and occasionally, no doubt, we decide to read love poetry or death poetry or an expressionistic play or short fiction dealing with suburbia. But more often we choose by author. We feel in a mood for Keats or Eugene O'Neill or Dickens, or we want to have another look at the Elizabethan sonneteers or at the ardent angularities of John Donne.

But we do not very often come to biography by thinking to ourselves: I want to read some Ludwig or some Maurois or some Marquis James. Rather, we desire to read a life of Napoleon or a life of Byron or a life of Andrew Jackson, or at least we choose according to categories of subjects: we have a hankering for medieval kings or nineteenth-century tycoons or Latin American adventurers.

The biographer does not regret this state of affairs; it is, indeed, the crown of his labors. The object of art, Horace reminds us, is to conceal art. The highest biographical art is the concealment of the biographer. Even Boswell illustrates this, for though he sometimes occupies space on the scene, he does so only to focus attention upon Johnson.

The other literary artists are unmistakably interfused in their work, identified with it. Despite stiff frowns from the new critics, we enjoy linking art with the artist. But we do not enjoy being aware of the biographer. Quite the contrary: being aware of the biographer spoils our illusion of sharing in a life. Unlike the poet, the biographer must have a talent for invisibility. Who would read the *Ode to a Nightingale* in order to learn about nightingales? Who would read a life of Napoleon for any other reason but to know Napoleon?

Current definitions of life-writing are lucid and simple, but not altogether satisfactory. In *The Development of English Biography*, Sir Harold Nicolson seeks for the essence of biography in classifying the motives which lead to its creation. Thus he excludes biographies written in order to celebrate the dead, didactic biography, like the lives of saints, and all biographies written for some special end or from some special viewpoint. He concludes that "pure" biography comes into being when the author, eschewing all extraneous purposes, writes the life of a man for its own sake, and, though adhering to truth, attempts to compose that life as a work of art.

In excluding the lives of saints or campaign biographies or pious memorials, Nicolson effectively clears the ground and takes us toward the heart of the matter. But can it be said that even the "purest" biographer is not moved by the commemorative urge? that he harbors, even if unconsciously, no didactic impulse? The barbaric yawp of an Assyrian King—his deeds and massacres preserved in stone—and the pawky Victorian eulogy are alike false to biography. But the fundamental emotion that powers biographical practice is surely the desire to mark, to keep alive, the passage of a man by recapturing the life of that man; what signals the pure biographer is that he regards the truth about a life as the only valid commemoration. Similarly, though the serious biographer eschews *overt* didacticism, it seems likely that he sweats over a life, say, of Henry James, not only because he regards James' life as suitable material for his art but also because that life, for him, says something or symbolizes something about the meaning of life in general that the writer is impelled to set forth.

Nicolson quotes approvingly the Oxford Dictionary's definition of biography—"The history of the lives of individual men as a branch of literature." In *The Nature of Biography*, John A. Garraty likewise defines biography as "the history of a human life" or "the record of a life." He explains, "It is thus a branch of history, each life a small segment in a vast mosaic . . ." But biography, as we have seen, is not a branch of history; for history is not a mosaic of lives, that is, a vast accumulation of biographical sketches, but a generalized narrative concerning events, movements, institutions. Thus the phrase "history of a life" is confused and misleading. The alternate definition offered by Mr. Garraty, "the record of a life" is not much more satisfactory. For record implies documentation, severely factual account, an objective marshaling of evidences, and no biography which hopes to recapture the sense of life being lived, to suggest the mysteries of personality, can be any of these things.

Biography is likewise often defined as "the story of a man's life." But "story" is as unsatisfactory in its way as "record." As "record" implies sheer fact, "story" implies fiction. Story leads us away from actuality.

But if biography is not the history or the record or the story of a man's life, what of a man's life is it? Considering that biography represents imagination limited by truth, facts raised to the power of revelation, I suggest that it may be defined as "the simulation, in words, of a man's life, from all that is known about that man."

This concept of life-writing goes back to James Boswell. In a letter to Bishop Percy he wrote, "It appears to me that mine is the best plan of biography that can be conceived; for my readers will, as near as may be, accompany Johnson in his progress, and, as it were, see each scene as it happened."

As the *simulation* in words of a life, biography works through effects, like the other literary arts; but it is an art with boundaries. The biographer, as Desmond McCarthy has felicitously pointed out, is "an artist upon oath." The definition excludes works at both ends of the biographical spectrum: the "fictionalized" biography simulates life but does not respect the materials at hand, whereas the fact-crammed biography, from the magpie school of scholarship-as-compilation, worships the materials at hand but does not simulate a life. The one fails truth; the other fails art. Between the two lies the impossible craft of true biography.

The shape of biography is partly created by the inner tensions peculiar to the practice. All great art achieves much of its force from tension, the exciting state of balance or reconciliation achieved among opposing elements. In painting there is obvious tension between form and color; in sculpture there is tension between the adamantine material and the plastic vi-

sion; in poetry there is tension between the violence of metaphor and the rigidity of meter.

Two characteristic tensions of biography arise out of the
relation between the biographer and his subject and out of the
conflict between the demands of simulation and the implaca-
bility of fact.

The question is often asked—how can a biographer be im-
partial (like a referee)? Of course, he cannot be so, would not
be so. He is not a biologist looking at one-celled animals under
the microscope, a curious but unmoved god. He is a human
being deeply involved with another human being. He lives
another life along with his own, and hopes he can persuade
the reader to live that life along with *his* own. A biography
may take a dozen years or more to write. Who would be
willing, who would be able to spend that much time with a
man for whom he had no feeling?

The biographer is forced into a struggle with his subject
which is, in a way, the opposite of the novelist's struggle. The
novelist must fight for detachment from material that is a part
of him, so that he may see that material in esthetic perspective,
may ask it the right questions. The biographer is already detached from his material, but it is an inert, a fortuitous detachment, a detachment that has not been won but thrust upon
him. Before he can achieve true detachment, he must first
achieve something like the psychic immersion in his material
that the novelist begins with.

In general, from the inception of modern life-writing in the
fifteenth century to the present, the biographer, and the autobiographer too, have confronted their subjects with a shar-
pening consciousness of perils and possibilities. As I shall try

to demonstrate in my final chapter, the deepening of psychological perception achieved in the twentieth century has affected the biographer's awareness of his relations with his materials as much as his understanding of the materials themselves.

A second, more obvious tension now develops between the subject, as brute materials, and the writer, as shaping intelligence; the conflict between the intransigence of facts and the imperious demand of art. It is this second tension that I have been mindful of in my definition of biography as the simulation, in words, of a life—but a simulation growing out of the materials at hand.

The researcher yearns to secure every scrap of paper left by a man's life; it is the artist who reminds him that he must stop somewhere—or death will take him as he stoops for yet another clue, and he will leave no mark of his struggles, except disorderly file boxes for his widow to dispose of. All the time that the biographer is collecting these scraps of paper, he must be doing something about them. At best, fact is harsh, recalcitrant matter, as tangible as the hunk of rusty iron one trips over and yet as shapeless as a paper hat in the rain. Fact is a cold stone, an inarticulate thing, dumb until something happens to it; and there is no use the biographer waiting for spontaneous combustion or miraculous alchemy. Fact must be rubbed up in the mind, placed in magnetic juxtaposition with other facts, until it begins to glow, to give off that radiance we call meaning. Fact is a biographer's only friend, and worst enemy.

This delicate adjustment between evidence and interpretation is partly determined by the way in which the biographer solves his problems, the problems indigenous to his material, and the general problems that confront all biographers. Like the other arts, biography has its cross-play of peculiar opportunities and dangers, and the quality of biography is largely determined by the biographer's ability to meet these challenges.

When biographers talk shop among themselves, you will hear animated discussions of a problem rarely mentioned by reviewers, the problem of gaps. That paper trail, extending from the birth certificate to the death certificate, is never continuous or complete. The more remote in time the man is, the more gaps there will be. These gaps occur at all stages in the trail but are very likely to come during the childhood and adolescence of the subject. One of the great triumphs of Boswell is the consummate biographical tact with which he resolved gaps. He spent less than a year—scattered over several years—in Johnson's company, and whereas he had masses of material for the later part of Johnson's life, he had comparatively thin materials for the earlier part. Yet he succeeds in giving the reader a sense of Johnson's life unfolding, a sense of that life being lived, from the beginning to the end.

There are no rules for handling gaps. Each paper trail is unlike any other paper trail. Each biographer is unlike any other biographer. The right way to fill gaps is unknown; the wrong ways are legion.[1]

---

[1] I recently chanced to look at four biographies of Francis Bacon: Charles Williams, *Bacon*, n.d.; Mary Sturt, *Francis Bacon*, 1932; Bryan Bevan, *The Real Francis Bacon*, 1960; Catherine Drinker Bowen, *Francis Bacon: The Temper of a Man*, 1963:

Little is known about Bacon's formative years: he went to Cambridge at thirteen; his later teens he spent in the train of the English ambassador to

Confronting a gap, the writer can but recognize that he is domesticated in imperfection; at the same time he must respond to King Harry's call—"Once more into the breach!"—and, summoning his talents and honesty, struggle to suggest the life of his man during the blank, without either pretending to more knowledge than he has or breaking the reader's illusion of a life unfolding.

I will use an experience of my own only because it is accessible. In trying to write a biography of Richard III, I was faced with an enormous gap in Richard's boyhood. From the age of ten till about fifteen (1462–66) he is but the merest supernumerary in the annals of the time. I could find only three elements out of which to build a bridge: what-was-going-on-in-England; what, in all probability, he was doing; where he was living.

Since Richard's brother, King Edward IV, and the mighty Kingmaker, Richard, Earl of Warwick, were in these years moving towards a collision in which Richard would be deeply involved, the great events of the period had to be intertwined in the texture of his life. I sought to introduce them, not from Richard's viewpoint—which would mean a leap into a mind

France; he then studied law at Gray's Inn. The writer has only about half a dozen biographical elements with which to fill this lamentable gap in Bacon's youth: information about his father, the Lord Keeper, and his mother; descriptions of the Bacon town and country houses; the state of learning at Cambridge; the political-cultural situation in France; life in the Inns of Court; and "background of the age." Each of the four biographers emphasizes one or more of these elements; it is not altogether clear, however, in the first three biographies whether that emphasis derives from quantity of material available, its attractiveness to the author, or its importance in Bacon's life. Mrs. Bowen steers the most decisive course by giving an over-all thematic significance to Bacon's youth, seeing it as the years of his "Eden," before he discovered, on the death of his father, that for all his high connections he would have to make his own way in the world.

closed to me—nor yet as inert information interrupting the biography, but as the stuff of Richard's developing experience.

As for the other elements, I had only the naked fact that Richard was being schooled as a "henxman," or page, in the household of the Earl of Warwick at Middleham Castle in Wensleydale, Yorkshire.

Out of several contemporary "courtesy books" and a mercifully detailed manual on the proper education for an aspirant knight, I sought to reconstruct the probable pattern of Richard's boyhood days. Place itself provided equally valuable clues. On the southern slope of Wensleydale—a great rift in the Yorkshire moors through which tumbles the river Ure —there stand the massive ruins of Middleham Castle. Behind, the land rolls up to the sky; before, stretch the village and the valley; then, empty moorland climbing to the clouds. It was in Richard's day a wild sweep of country, inhabited by a folk more primitive than those in Edward IV's capital, marked by huge stone abbeys and bristling castles, the hills rounded by the stamp of Celtic kings and Roman legions. Since, in later years, Richard owned Middleham and spent his happiest days there, I concluded that he must have developed his feeling for the region during his early sojourn. I therefore juxtaposed his training in knighthood with an account of Wensleydale and its people in an attempt to suggest the shape of his boyhood.

The problem of filling gaps involves more than material; it is likewise a question of rhythm. Obviously, the amount of biographical space-time devoted to a moment in the subject's life should approximate the weight of significance of the moment. Not only, then, must the writer find material in the things that stand around, in order to bridge space; he must likewise sensitively adjust the movement of the narrative so that its pace reflects the true pace of the life. Otherwise, even the least perceptive reader will feel that "something is wrong," perhaps that the biography is "dry" or that the biographer has somehow cheated him or that he has missed a point. When the narrative moves quickly or slowly according to the quantity of the material rather than the quality of the experience, the writer *and* his subject have become prisoners of the papers.

It is gaps that tempt the fledgling biographer to speculate, the "artistic" biographer to invent, the scholarly biographer to give a lecture on history. To fill gaps by wondering aloud, lying, padding—or simply to leave them for the reader to tumble into—is not to fill the shoes of a true biographer.

If the absence of witnesses—gaps—poses one of the chief biographical problems, availability of witnesses does not mean that the biographer can switch on the automatic pilot. Mark Schorer has eloquently commented on the vanity, fallibility, unconscious duplicity, animosity, taciturnity or volubility of living witnesses and evoked the specter of libel rustling above the workbench of the biographer writing of a man recently deceased, like Sinclair Lewis.

Dead witnesses, preserved only as paper, are no less humanly perverse, inaccurate, and prejudiced; and if they have been dead for more than two centuries, their terseness, their indifference to details of behavior, their maddening penchant for generalizing, moralizing, and sometimes paralyzing human situations, in sum, their over-all failure to satisfy the most modest demands of twentieth-century curiosity, offer perhaps even greater obstacles to biography than the copiousness, however misleading, of the witness-in-the-flesh.

This brief sketch of some of the enigmas that beset the biographical workshop is no place for a discussion of the lenses to be employed in the scrutiny of evidences. Rules have been promulgated in a few manuals of life-writing, but I suspect that they represent not so much an analytic account of the battle in progress as a picture of the terrain after the dead have been buried, the field tidied, and historical markers erected. The bald truth is, however "scientifically" the biographer tries to quiz his witnesses, he is often sloppy, intuitive, temerarious, doubt-ridden, and hopeful, his intellect clouded by visceral irrelevancies and glandular dreams. In short, he is a frail mortal, on a very mortal mission, measuring other frail mortals. If he pretends to be a microscope, the damned specimen evaporates.

Judicial, scientific, historical tests of evidence are useful, but the writer who deals in the unstable stuff of letters, diary, conversations, hearsay, the elusiveness of human testimony not offered as testimony, evidences that may yield more in their lies, omissions, euphemisms, and periphrases than in their truths, mainly depends on his shaky knowledge of psychology, his own sense of human nature, what he has learned from other biographers, dogged industry, a skepticism that is quizzical rather than systematic, and a determination to reject the golden fable for the leaden fact.

The biographer does not trust his witnesses, living or dead. He may drip with the milk of human kindness, believe everything that his wife and his friends and his children tell him, enjoy his neighbors and embrace the universe—but in the workshop he must be as ruthless as a board meeting smelling out embezzlement, as suspicious as a secret agent riding the Simplon-Orient express, as cold-eyed as a pawnbroker viewing a leaky concertina. With no respect for human dignity, he plays off his witnesses one against the other, snoops for additional information to confront them with, probes their prejudices and their pride, checks their reliability against their self-interest, thinks the worst until he is permitted to think better. Withal, he must expect to be deceived, and more than once, and thus stand ready, unto page-proof, to excise the much tested truth that turns out to be error or invention.

The biographer attempting to make sense out of the imperfect paper trail, brooding over gaps and gabble, is like a man sitting at a bizarre play. He knows the "plot" and the cast of characters, and he understands substantially what is going to happen. His mission, however, is to report the drama in detail; of which the performance he is witnessing is a flawed and sometimes zany simulacrum.

Happenings explode on the stage without warning; happenings are prepared for and fail to occur; supporting players pop up with nothing to do and disappear into the wings when most needed. The protagonist is supposed to be always on stage; but he sometimes vanishes, even in the middle of a speech, or crawls into a corner when the script clearly calls for him to stand front and center, or exhibits inexplicable postures of agony or joy, or at a critical moment falls suddenly silent. Actions move toward a climax which is cut off by a descending curtain; important exchanges between characters take place behind the furniture; and on occasion the subsidiary actors maliciously mask the protagonist and carry on a Hamletless *Hamlet*.

Sometimes the biographer cannot hear; sometimes he cannot see; sometimes he cannot understand what he does hear and see. Yet, by means of this performance he must recreate the play—without inventing anything and without altering the plot.

Another of the great biographical problems is the management of time. A novel usually pictures only a segment of life; the novelist shuttles forward and backward in time in order to enrich that segment; the fictional character is a creature of the novelist's time. But a person is a creature of actual time; we must be able to share with him not only the grand human chronology of growth, maturity, death, but also lesser patterns of sequential experience, small half-hidden cumulations of behavior from which emerge new tendrils of relationship between the man and his world.

In the earlier drafts of a biography of King Louis XI on which I am still working, I succumbed to a fictional device for the opening. The shape of the materials themselves and the opportunity to sketch immediately the chief theme of Louis' youth prompted me to manipulate time like a novelist.

Not until his thirteenth year, as a bridegroom, does Louis make a sustained appearance in history. Contemporary chronicles describe the wedding in sufficient detail so that I could mould the materials into a scene, place Louis at the center of a cluster of moments. Even better, the behavior of Louis' father, Charles VII, at the ceremony revealed his hostility toward the boy; and it was a bitter antagonism between father and son that was to shape Louis' whole life as Dauphin.

Thus, by beginning with Louis at thirteen instead of at birth, I plunged the reader at once into a life being lived, and provided a focus for the first twelve years of his life—which I then recounted—in the unspoken question: what had caused, so early, bad feeling between King and Dauphin?

Though doubts soon assailed me, I clung to this pretty opening through several drafts. No use: I had to junk it. A character in a novel inhabits a time-dimension invented by the author and has no existence apart from it. A person, however, has his own time-dimension, quite independent of a biographer's ingenuity. In rupturing Louis' time to impose my own, I was turning him into a fictional being, I was overtly staging rather than unfolding a life.

So Louis himself kept imperiously reminding me. I was, he told me, foisting on the public *my* Louis instead of him, *the* Louis. Furthermore, I was cutting him off from his common humanity: like other human beings he began as a baby, not as a bridegroom. He declared rudely that if I had so little confidence in his identity as an acutal person, there was no use my trying to accompany him through a lifetime.

I have let him have his way: he begins by being born, and I end a little wiser. Biographical time and novelistic time do not mix.

Yet biography is the simulation, not the ledger-book, of an existence. The biographer cannot reproduce the actual concatenation of events. His subject may, over a period of months, be developing a dozen different themes of experience; if the biographer attempts to thread the tangle of details day by day out of which these experiences are being built he will conjure up chaos. He must thrust into the reader's ears the noisy cross-currents of man's passage through time, wet his tongue with the salty murk of reality; but if he is to make that passage intelligible, he must do violence to time: the clutter of events will be cut away, happenings scattered through years will be grouped, in order to reveal underlying currents of behavior.

Certain continuing sounds in the "buzz and hum" of daily life—a hobby, an eccentricity of diet, a habitual inability to stay awake at lectures, a desultory friendship too important to omit but insufficiently substantial to be woven through—will almost of necessity be grouped arbitrarily and brought into the narrative when the biographer's ear tells him that the moment has struck. The chief purpose of "groupings," how-ever, is to elicit—but not to diagram—the master-themes of a life: patterns of hopes and illusions, preoccupations, fears, rhythmic movements of character discernible in the diurnal stream of existence, grand designs of personality expressed as behavior.

Yet thematic groupings cannot be permitted to block or deform the sweep of chronology, the sequential heart-beat of a life, the "faring onward" of our tragi-comic journey. They cannot be deployed like the topics of an expository essay—exposition is the enemy of biography, dead tissue cumbering a living organism. They must suggest a life moving through time, not the writer's capacity for tidiness. James Parton, the first American professional biographer, put the matter practi-cally: "A good thing is twice as good if it comes in at the right place."

Suetonius and Plutarch, working in the narrow compass of sketch, or profile, developed a biographical mode in which thematic grouping and the unfolding of time interpenetrated each other in a stylized arrangement of life-materials. Certain present-day biographers, as we shall see in the final chapter, have sauced the device of "grouping" with psychoanalysis and novelistic legerdemain as if human chronology were as boneless as an oyster and a man's life so much mud to be arbitrarily patted into cakes.

The absence, or the prevalence, of witnesses, gaps and traps in the paper trail, the management of time, and the eliciting of patterns are some of the most difficult challenges confronting a biographer. I will mention but one more, the problem of balancing the time-viewpoint of the subject and the time-viewpoint of the biographer. It is easy to see that what is the unknown future for the subject is the well-known past for the biographer; and it is easy to say that the biographer must use the advantage of this difference but not take advantage of it.

In practice, however, the distinction between recreating and commenting on a life is not so easy to respect. And the distinction is one that must be dealt with at the most critical moments in the life, the moments of decision, the moment when career takes a turn or love takes a wife, the moment when character is simultaneously illustrated and reshaped by a choice of action or attitude. These are the moments, sometimes not simple to detect, which mark the true stages of existence, the determining and determinate climaxes summing up the past and giving birth to the future, the moments when, as Carlyle pointed out, a man (and his biographer) discovers what he is in what he does.

Inevitably, then, the biographer seeks to choose, in the welter of psychological-physical happenings leading toward such a moment, those elements which will be crucial in the subject's decision, as, after the moment, he must bring into the foreground those elements which show the working out of the decision. To such an extent the biographer, thanks to his vantage point in time, can comment upon the life.

But biographers are sometimes tempted to comment overtly on the decision itself, before it is made, after it is made, even as it is being made. They shout at Napoleon that he must not send Grouchy in pursuit of Blucher, at Hamilton that he had better steer clear of Burr, at James that it is idle for him to attempt the drama, at Antony that he is foolish to fight by sea, at Ben Jonson that he should not try to compose classical tragedy—and the deafened reader cannot hear what is actually going on, is jerked away from the subject to the biographer; indeed, the deafened reader is likely to conclude, perhaps unfairly, that the biographer is arrogantly pluming himself on a prescience that has no more merit than the good luck of being born considerably later than his subject.

If the biographer is to create the sense of a life being lived, he cannot leap from his own time into his subject's time to nudge the poor man in the ribs or make faces at his deliberations, like Faustus playing tricks on the Pope. The grand dimension of every man's life is the opacity of the future. The biographer, if he has foresight, will exercise the willing suspension of hindsight.

Biography attempts the simulation, in words, of a man's life, from what is known about that life, from the paper trail, the enigmatic footprint. Thus it differs from other literary arts. They seek to evoke reality from illusion; biography hopes to fasten illusion upon reality, to elicit, from the coldness of paper, the warmth of a life being lived.

II

Looking Back:
Biography in Antiquity
and the Middle Ages

For the purposes of this brief survey, I will include autobiographical composition as a close relative, or specialized form, of biography. Autobiography works by somewhat different principles and offers a somewhat different satisfaction from biography; but it *is* life-writing, it is the life of a man which happens to be written by himself. Like biography, it presents a wide range of expression, bounded on the one side by the psychological or spiritual autobiography so concentrated on the soul that the outward world and the life being lived in it are but a blur, and on the other by the memoir or reminiscence, in which the writer records those manifestations of the world—people, places, events—which most deeply penetrated his memory, and remains himself a hazy being. Between *who is remembering* and *what is remembered* lies the *res gestae*, the

29

unreflective record of experiences.

Paradoxically, though the autobiographer enjoys a far more intimate knowledge of his subject than the biographer, he usually produces a life that is neither so rounded, so complete, nor so close to the actual life as the biographer's. Both aim at recapturing a person in his journey through time, but the biographer recreates the life out of evidences, whereas the autobiographer recreates it out of memory—and memory, unlike paper remains, is plastic, is itself creative. The autobiographer gives us a special truth: a life as reshaped by recollection, with all of recollection's conscious and unconscious omissions, distortions, and illusions. Autobiography is not the true picture of a life; it is a true picture of what, at one moment of the life, the subject wishes, and is impelled, to reveal of that life. For this reason, of all the materials available to the biographer, autobiographical writings are the most dangerous, the most difficult, and the most exciting to handle.

The autobiographer, in sum, knows more but tells less, *on the whole*, than the biographer—granted that no biographer could attempt, much less achieve, the portrait of Augustine's spiritual struggle which, *for certain moments of his life* Augustine creates in his *Confessions*. The autobiographer regenerates his materials even as he uses them. What a journal kept in youth reports and what the autobiographer presents in recollection are likely to be quite different. Far from lending authenticity to his narrative, direct quotation from letter or diary is very apt to spoil it by violating the shaping viewpoint of the work and by confusing the reader with contradictory truths.

Autobiography is life-writing, with a difference. Gibbon

declares, ". . . I must be conscious that no one is so well qualified as myself to describe the series of my thoughts and actions." Let us call upon Cowley for an answer: "It is a hard and nice subject for a man to write of himself; it grates his own heart to say anything of disparagement and the reader's ears to hear anything of praise from him."

Quite a good case can be made out, however, for the proposition that autobiography has given as many famous works of literature to the world as biography.

From the early centuries of the first millennium B.C. to the extinguishing of the Western Empire in the fifth century A.D. there is a steady hum of autobiographical and biographical activity in the Graeco-Roman world. Much of the work is lost; much is fragmentary; and much of what remains suggests that the loss is not grievous, except as historical record. Roughly speaking, during the first thousand of these fifteen hundred years the biographical impulse took the form of funeral elegies, political orations, rhetorical and philosophical exercises which were largely concerned with individuals as representing ideal types of character or ethical patterns of culture. During the last third of this period, from Augustus to Attila, biographical writing exhibits the same declining energies or the same increasing subservience to alien ends that appears in the other literary arts.

There is, then, little life-writing, in our sense of the word. On the other hand, that little consists of masterpieces. Biography makes its appearance among western mankind not like a swaddling child but in majesty: it begins with the two greatest personalities of antiquity—or should it be said that the two greatest personalities of antiquity begin with biography? The collision of Socrates with the world, the collision of Jesus of Nazareth with the world, shake biography into being.

There is no knowing whether Plato adheres to biographical truth, as we conceive it today, though what we learn of Socrates from other sources, like Xenophon's *Memorabilia*, allows us to suppose so; and he does not give us anything like a complete life. In his two consummate biographical Dialogues, however, the *Apology* and the *Phaedo*, he recreates the last days of Socrates so artfully that they have ever since held empery over the imaginations of men. The trial of Socrates in the *Apology* and the account of his death in the *Phaedo* reveal the life in its moments of transcendent achievement and lay bare the ultimate reaches of the character. Plato, great artist as well as thinker, recognized when the man outsoared the mind. In these dialogues he relinquishes the figure he had used systematically as a philosophical tool and, turning biographer, evokes an extraordinary personality at the pitch of its power, a force breaking through system into poetry.

Some four centuries later, there came into being four Lives of Jesus of Nazareth, works whose profound biographical originality have been inevitably obscured by their religious significance. They are the first approaches to authentic biography to be produced in the ancient world—called into existence, not altogether unlike the *Apology* and *Phaedo*, by a revolutionary alteration of human attitudes. Their object is to propagate a faith, to present man-as-God—an object not encouraging to biography—but by their accumulations of homely detail, their use of anecdote and dialogue, their emphasis on feeling, their depiction of personality in crisis, they thrust us into the living texture of a life.

By the beginning of the second century A.D., not long after the Gospels came into being, life-writing for its own sake and in its own image finally appears. The three great biographers of the pagan Roman world do their work in the same historical context: Plutarch, born about 50 A.D.; Tacitus, born a few years later; and Suetonius, born about 75 A.D.

Like the portrait of Pericles in the *Peloponnesian War* of Thucydides, Tacitus' most famous biographical piece, his account of the Emperor Tiberius, forms part of a history, his *Annals*. In his Life of his father-in-law, Agricola, however, he produces a complete, finely wrought biography, which is not so well known, probably because it has something of the marmoreal quality of statuary and concentrates on the Roman administrator rather than on the man.

Plutarch and Suetonius also reflect their cultural milieu— Rome, exemplifying the arts of government and the virtues of statesmanship, apparently at the farthest stretch of imperial greatness but, in fact, already in decline. They both deal with rulers and men of state; they create their Lives within the compass of the profile or biographical sketch; and they alternate movement through time with illustrations of personality, emphasizing thematic grouping of biographical elements rather than the chronological unfolding of character.

Plutarch has been too often and too well praised to require comment here. Though he sets his contrasted lives of famous Greeks and Romans in an ethical framework, dwelling upon the virtues of man as governor, he possesses a wonderful flair for suggesting character in action and for lifting his materials onto the plane of drama. His gifts as a literary artist enable him to exceed his purpose as a philosopher.

The third member of the trio, Gaius Suetonius Tranquillus, has not fared nearly so well as Plutarch in critical estimation, at least in our day. Twentieth-century critics nag and cluck at Suetonius because, one gathers, he lacks the high seriousness and exquisite sense of art their palates demand. Perhaps they thus redeem their low pleasure in reading him. But if as a literary artist Suetonius is inferior to Plutarch, if his work lacks the gloss of Plutarch's writing and the nice projection of character in beautifully arranged moments, on the other hand, Suetonius is more the essential biographer, the biographer in blood and nerves, than Plutarch.

He has no ethical purpose; he has curiosity. As secretary to the Emperor Hadrian, he possessed access to rich sources, and he grubs and digs in order to mine the essential stuff of character. He instinctively recognizes the telling detail, quotes the revealing letter, picks out the characteristic turns of speech that recreate the man for us. He projects in his *Lives of the Twelve Caesars* a biographical panorama that has ever since delighted mankind.

One of the few pieces of information, or pseudo-information, that has come down to us about Suetonius is that the Emperor Hadrian finally fired him because he did not pay proper respect to the Empress. Perhaps he could not altogether sink the biographer in the courtier, and she caught him studying her with a disconcertingly unawed gaze. He was an inquirer into, not a respecter of, persons.

Plutarch's life of Julius Caesar is more dramatic than Suetonius', but Suetonius has good things of his own. After Caesar had been stabbed, he writes, "All the conspirators made off, and he lay there lifeless for some time, until finally three common slaves put him on a litter and carried him home, with one arm hanging down." That unforgettable arm is the hallmark of Suetonius' genius.

He catches Augustus' personality in the flavor of idiom. "That in his everyday conversation he used certain favorite and peculiar expressions appears from letters in his own hand. . . . Urging his correspondent to put up with present circumstances, such as they are, he says: 'Let's be satisfied with the Cato we have'; and to express the speed of a hasty action, 'Quicker than you can cook asparagus.' I have also observed this special peculiarity in his manner of writing: he does not divide words or carry superfluous letters from the end of one line to the beginning of the next, but writes them just below the rest of the word and draws a loop around them."

In a series of flashing glimpses, like a motion picture, Suetonius stamps upon our imaginations that monster and madman, Caligula. "He used to say," Suetonius writes, "that there was nothing in his own character which he admired and approved more highly than what he called his immovable rigor. . . . When he was on the point of killing his brother, and suspected that he had taken drugs as a precaution against poison, he cried: 'What! An antidote against Caesar?' . . . He seldom had anyone put to death except by numerous slight wounds. 'Strike so that he may feel that he is dying,' was his constant order . . ." We see the madman caught in the horror of his own madness: "Weary of lying in bed wide awake during the greater part of the night, he would now sit upon his couch, and now wander through the long colonnades, crying out from time to time for daylight and longing for its coming."

Here is the impulsiveness and disconcerting lack of dignity of the emperor Claudius—"When a debate was going on about the butchers and vintners, he cried out in the House: 'Now, pray, who can live without a snack,' and then went on to describe the abundance of the old taverns to which he himself used to go for wine in earlier days."

As for sustained biographical narrative, Suetonius' account of the death of Nero is hardly excelled, perhaps, in the whole range of life-writing:

> In the meanwhile, when word came that the other armies had revolted, he tore to pieces the dispatches which were handed to him as he was dining, tipped over the table, and dashed to the ground two favorite drinking cups, which he called 'Homeric' because they were carved with scenes from Homer's poems. Then taking some poison from Locusta and putting it into a golden box, he crossed over into the Servilian gardens, where he tried to induce the Tribunes and Centurions of the Guard to accompany him in his flight, first sending his most trustworthy freedmen to Ostia, to get a fleet ready. But when some gave evasive answers and some openly refused, one even cried:
>
> > 'Is it, then, such a dreadful thing, to die?'
> > [Vergil, *Aeneid*, XII, 646]
>
> Whereupon he turned over various plans in his mind, whether to go as a suppliant to the Parthians or to Galba, or to appear to the people on the rostra, dressed in black, and beg as pathetically as he could for pardon for his past offenses; and if he could not soften their hearts, to entreat them at least to allow him the prefecture of Egypt. After-

wards a speech composed for this purpose was found in his
writing desk. But it is thought that he did not dare to deliver
it for fear of being torn to pieces before he could reach the
Forum.

Having therefore put off further consideration to the following day, he awoke about midnight and finding that the
guard of soldiers had left, he sprang from his bed and sent
for all his friends. Since no reply came back from any one, he
went himself to their rooms with a few followers. But finding that all the doors were closed and that no one replied to
him he returned to his own chamber, from which now the
very caretakers had fled, taking with them even the bed-
clothing and the box of poison. Then he at once called for
the gladiator Spiculus or any other skillful killer at whose
hand he might find death, and when no one appeared, he cried
'Have I then neither friend nor foe?' and ran out as if to
throw himself into the Tiber.

Changing his purpose again, he sought for some retired
place, where he could hide and collect his thoughts. And
when his freedman Phaon offered his villa in the suburbs between the Via Nomentana and the Via Salaria near the fourth
milestone, just as he was, barefooted and in his tunic, he put
on a faded cloak, covered his head, and holding a handker-
chief before his face, mounted a horse with only four attend-
ants, one of whom was Sporus. At once he was startled by a
shock of earthquake and a flash of lightning full in his face,
and he heard the shouts of the soldiers from the camp hard
by, as they prophesied destruction for him and success for
Galba. He also heard one of the wayfarers whom he met
say: 'These men are after Nero,' and another ask: 'Is there
anything new in the city about Nero?' Then his horse took
fright at the smell of a corpse which had been thrown out
into the road, his face was exposed, and a retired soldier of
the Guard recognized him and saluted him. When they
came to a by-path leading to the villa, they turned the horses

loose and he made his way amid bushes and brambles and along a path through a thicket of weeds to the back wall of the house, with great difficulty and only when a robe was thrown down for him to walk on. Here the aforesaid Phaon urged him to hide for a time in a pit, from which sand had been dug, but he declared that he would not go under ground while still alive, and after waiting for a while until a secret entrance into the villa could be made, he scooped up in his hand some water to drink from a pool close by, saying: 'This is Nero's distilled water.' Then, as his cloak had been torn by the thorns, he pulled out the twigs which had pierced it, and crawling on all fours through a narrow passage that had been dug, he entered the villa and lay down in the first room he came to, on a couch with a common mattress, over which an old cloak had been thrown. Though suffering from hunger and renewed thirst, he refused some coarse bread which was offered him, but drank a little lukewarm water.

At last, while his companions one and all urged him to save himself as soon as possible from the indignities that threatened him, he bade them dig a grave in his presence, proportioned to the size of his own person, collect any bits of marble that could be found, and at the same time bring water and wood for presently disposing of his body. As each of these things was done, he wept and said again and again: 'What an artist the world is losing!'

While he hesitated, a letter was brought to Phaon by one of his couriers. Nero snatching it from his hand read that he had been pronounced a public enemy by the Senate, and that they were seeking to punish him in the ancient fashion. And he asked what manner of punishment that was. When he learned that the criminal was stripped naked, fastened by the neck in a forked stake and then beaten to death with rods, in mortal terror he seized two daggers which he had brought with him, and then, after trying the point of each, put them

up again, pleading that the fated hour had not yet come.
Now he would beg Sporus to begin to lament and wail, and
now entreat some one to help him take his life by setting
him the example. Anon he reproached himself for his cow-
ardice in such words as these: 'To live despoiled, disgraced—
this does not become Nero, does not become him—one
should be resolute at such times—come, rouse thyself!' And
now the horsemen were at hand who had orders to take him
off alive. When he heard them, he quavered:

> 'The trampling of swift-footed studs is in my ear,'
> [*Iliad*, X, 535]

and drove a dagger into his throat, aided by Epaphroditus,
his private secretary. He was all but dead when a Centurion
rushed in, and as he placed a cloak to the wound, pretending that he had come to aid him, Nero merely gasped: 'Too
late!' and 'This is fidelity!' With these words he was gone,
his eyes so set and starting fom their sockets that all who saw
him shuddered with horror.

Dismissed by several modern critics as "a mere compiler,"
or "a gossip," as lacking historical perspective and literary
graces and high ethical considerations, Suetonius remains one
of the world's great biographers. In his *Lives of the Twelve
Caesars* he "brings 'em back alive." It is his one virtue, but in
biography that is the only virtue.

The remaining centuries of the Roman Empire, with the
ebbing of pagan literature and the rising tide of Christian,
produced only one work of serious biographical interest, the
Confessions of Augustine. Here we find arrestingly conjoined
the inheritance of the psychological awareness achieved by
Roman civilization, a revolutionary assessment of experience,
and a most powerful, indeed imperious, personality. The re-

sult is a work that explosively signals the shift in human attitudes caused by the spread of Christianity and offers brilliant
moments of self-revelation.

Yet the *Confessions*, for all their originality, their psychological force, the astonishing analysis of the transformation of
a personality, are something less, if something more, than genuine autobiography. They narrow the scope of life to those
instances when the individual reacts to the bidding of a superior power, and thus, fundamentally, they present a *type* of
soul-struggle and a ruthlessly specialized variation of existence
rather than the conflict of a single being with his world. The
Confessions are a sociological-psychological-religious document of enduring influence but as autobiography they have
been somewhat overrated. Indeed, in picturing an essential
process of redemption, the pattern of the making of a Christian soul, they lead, historically, to an antithesis of life-
writing, the hardening and attenuating of human experience
into an exemplum to convert the heathen or to confirm the
faithful.

The ancient world did not develop a strong biographical
tradition, but in its chief biographical works can be perceived
three principal modes of life-writing that have persisted to
this day: first, biography springing from a relationship in life
between subject and writer, as exemplified in the *Apology*
and *Phaedo*, Tacitus' *Agricola*, and the four Gospels (at least
based on materials arising from life-relationships); second,
biography resulting from the pressure of talent and inclina-
tion, professional biography, as practiced by Plutarch and
Suetonius; third, biography produced to satisfy the require-
ments or the predilections of an age, to act as a beast of

burden for ends other than the illumination of a life, what we might call demand-biography, all too vigorously illustrated by the last days of the Empire. In the twilight of the pagan world courtiers generated feeble panegyrics of emperors in a parody of Suetonius, while the flooding light of Christianity bleached the biographical impulse into propagandizing tracts, the celebration of miracle-workers and martyrs.

What follows is the long reign of demand-biography: a thousand years of saints' lives.

By peering carefully into this darkness of hagiography which endured from about 400 to 1400, we can espy glimmerings of life-writing—in Eadmer's *Life of Anselm*, details of the Archbishop's boyhood and snatches of his talk; in Joinville's *Life of St. Louis* (Louis IX of France), lively bits of human portraiture; in Abelard's *History of My Calamities*, moments of poignant self-revelation; and other faint lights here and there. These glimmerings have all been explored in standard histories of biography. To dwell upon them is but making do in the desert, an exercise in fortitude.

There are two works, however, which deserve attention, if only because one of them is unknown to biographical history and the other is, I think, generally undervalued. They signal the persistence of genuine biographical impulse in the darkest reaches of the early Middle Ages, but they are much more than historical curiosities—their voices carry clear and strong across the centuries.

The first of these works, the *History of the Franks* by Bishop Gregory of Tours, comes out of the very beginnings of the western world, crude and violent sixth-century Gaul a generation after Clovis had there established the Frankish kingdom. Gregory himself painfully reveals the prime psychological effect of Rome's decay and final plunge into barbarism: the terrible shrinkage of self-awareness, the closing down of mental horizons.

Gregory came of a distinguished Gallo-Roman family, was gently reared, and given the best education of the day. By administrative talents and a commanding personality, he won his way to the coveted bishopric of Tours, at a time when a bishop shared with the Count of the district the responsibilities of government, such as it was in that wild age. One of the most civilized and able men of all Gaul, then—how terribly primitive he is, how constricted in his outlook. He hated Arian Christians worse than the devil; he saw skull-splitting, treacherous Clovis as a dweller in heaven because Clovis had turned Christian; he writes numerous saints' lives saturated in miracle; he believed that no doctor could prescribe for the body a medicine one-tenth so potent as a pinch of dust or a bit of fringe from a saint's tomb. He was so sunk in superstition that even a monk of the tenth century—a period not noted for breadth of view—found him barbarically credulous.

His *History of the Franks*, in ten books, begins with the creation of the world and proceeds, in the first three books, to the mid-sixth century by a feeble copying of the works of late Roman historians. Then occurs a magical change.

As one of the chief bishops of Gaul, Gregory was plunged into the very heart of his age—diplomat, governor, politician of church and state, an adviser, sometimes an opponent, of kings. When he begins to recount events out of his own experience, his pen suddenly leaps into life. The last seven books of the *History* are of his times and the part he played in them.

Frequently missing the significance of what is going on but unfailingly sensitive to personalities and the drama of life, he spreads before us a galaxy of furious saints and flamboyant sinners: from a moldy zealot crying the end of the world to Count Rauching, who lights his banquet-room by fastening candles to the shins of his slaves in order to enjoy their sufferings while he dines; from loyal and upright Duke Lupus and the brilliant, unscrupulous general, Mummolus, invincible except against his own ambition, to that turbulent Bishop of Gap, Sagittarius, who, delighting in war, beat his foes to death with a leaden maul so that he could not be held guilty of shedding Christian blood.

Against this panorama of untamed human vitality Gregory limns, in crude bold strokes, the great personages of the age, the grandsons of Clovis and their queens, all of whom he knew well. In the whole subsequent history of the West, it would be difficult to find a quintet of rulers of men, an involvement of five destinies, so pungent as these, so illustrative of the strange reaches and passionate depths of human behavior—and it is Gregory's life-writing that gives them their being:

"Good King Guntram" of Burgundy, affable and bewildered, groping to be a man of goodwill in a time of terror, given to rages of frustration quickly appeased, becomes, following the deaths of his brothers, the Benevolent Uncle of the era and, after his own death—despite a few thoughtless murders—a saint.

Sigebert, King of Austrasia, almost a hero out of saga, the

barbarian chieftain at his best, sought dignity for the House
of Clovis in marrying a beautiful cultured Visigothic Princess,
Brunehild, and died on poisoned blades prepared by a brother's wife.

Sigebert's queen, Brunehild, indomitably ambitious, fought,
despite the fierce opposition of the Frankish nobles, to shore
up the remains of Roman civilization, and in consequence was
one day dragged to her death at the tail of a camel.

Chilperic, King of Neustria, the most complex and psychologically interesting of the quintet, hated—and misunderstood
—by Gregory, who brands him "the Herod and Nero of his
time," was caught in the toils of a fatal passion for a savage
serving-wench, Fredegund ("the enemy of God and man,"
Gregory calls her), whom he made his queen and who
twisted his life into tragic courses. An unstable and strangely
sensitive personality struggling within the skin of a barbarian,
Chilperic had a wonderful flair for gesture: curiously or quiz-
zically—or fearfully, as Gregory thinks—he left a blank sheet
of paper on the tomb of St. Martin to find out if that most
powerful of saints would vouchsafe him a message; and
when Guntram and Sigebert threatened war, he dramatized
his disdain of them by building arenas and presiding over cir-
cus games at Soissons and Paris. He was a desperate seeker in
the darkness of a world growing darker, trying to adjust the
Roman alphabet to Germanic sounds, to write poetry, to revive the arts of metalworking, to find some meaning for his
life.

Despite his shortcomings in narrative, Gregory understands
the value of dramatized moments in life-writing; he shapes
scenes that lay bare more of character in action than he some-

times perceives, particularly since, as warranty for their truth, he often puts himself on the stage.

The most famous conflict between Gregory and Chilperic occurred when an assembly of bishops were trying Praetextatus, the Bishop of Rouen, on a charge of *lèse-majesté* and perjury. In the first session Gregory spoke out against the accusation, though most of the bishops were afraid to cross Chilperic's will—particularly since the fearsome Fredegund, out for blood, was urging her husband on.

Gregory continues, "Two sycophants among them, it is lamentable to say it of bishops, went to the king and told him that there was no greater enemy of his interests than myself. Forthwith one from the court was sent with all speed to command my presence. When I arrived, the king was standing near an arbor formed of branches, with Bishop Bertram on his right and Ragnemod upon his left [supporters of Chilperic]: before them was a bench covered with bread and various dishes.

"As soon as he saw me, the king said: 'O bishop, it is thy part freely to deal justice to all, and lo! I receive not justice at thy hands; but I see thee consenting with iniquity, and in thee is fulfilled the proverb that crow picketh not out crow's eye.'

"Whereto I answered: 'If any among us, O king, would overstep the path of justice, it is in thy power to correct him; but if thou transgress, who may rebuke thee?'

"He replied (for his flatterers had inflamed him against me): 'All other men show me justice; with thee alone I find it not. . . . I will call together the people of Tours, and I will say to them: "Cry aloud against Gregory, that he is unjust and accordeth justice to no man." And when they shout as I bid, I shall make answer to them: "Myself, the king, can find no justice at his hands, and how shall ye lesser folk find it?" ' "

Gregory answered that his conscience was clear and that if the people cried out against him, everybody would know that it was because of Chilperic's urging. He reminded the king that he had only to consult the law and the canons to find out the truth of the case. "Then, as if to propitiate me, deeming that I did not see through his crafty dealing, he turned to a dish placed before him, and said: 'These dishes I have had prepared for thee; there is nothing in this but fowl and a little pulse . . .' "

We may well feel that Gregory does not minimize his own courageous independence in recreating this scene from memory, and that Chilperic hardly seems the violent despot whom Gregory is fond of denouncing. Looking over Gregory's shoulder, we sense Chilperic's love of play-acting, his enjoyment of irony, even his capacity to charm: Gregory ends the scene by reporting, "After this I accepted some bread, and even drank wine before I went away."

Gregory does not grasp the chief political movement of the day, the attempt of the nobles to thwart the development of royal power. He even fails to see as a coherent pattern the theatrical struggle between those mortal foes, the widowed queens Fredegund and Brunehild, with poor Guntram of Burgundy uncomfortably trying to placate them, like a man tiptoeing between a volcano and a tidal wave. Gregory does not always succeed in following elementary sequences of developing event and interplays of cause-and-effect. He does not know how to write a memoir or shape the biographies that lie within it.

Yet, despite these enormous faults and lacks, he has the true instincts of a biographer; his native talent triumphs over his limitations. However crudely, he is able to bring home to paper the living texture of his experience—the "mighty beasts of the Merovingian jungle." Blinkered though he was by superstition and ecclesiastical bias, he could not help being fascinated by the sheer display of human nature. A hunter who cannot dress meat for a table, he nonetheless knows how to beat the twilight thickets and bring in the game. The *History of the Franks* is much more than a biographical glimmering; it is something of a biographical miracle.

Three hundred years after Gregory wrote his history, there appears, mysteriously, a self-conscious work of biography. It represents the conjunction of two remarkable men—the Frankish ruler Charlemagne, who made himself the Emperor of the West, and a cleric at his court named Einhard. Unlike Gregory, Einhard did have a model for his *Life of Charlemagne:* he knew Suetonius' *Lives of the Twelve Caesars,* and he followed Suetonius' general method in order to give form to the work. But what is most noteworthy in his *Life of Charlemagne* owes nothing to Suetonius.

Einhard recognizes that the biographer is an artist with an obligation and with a point of view and he feels bound to disclose these to the reader. "I have been careful," he writes in his preface, "not to omit any facts that could come to my knowledge, but at the same time not to offend by a prolix style those minds that despise everything modern. . . . I see no reason why I should refrain from entering upon a task of this kind, since no man can write with more accuracy than I of events that took place about me, and of facts concerning which I had personal knowledge, ocular demonstration, as the saying goes, and I have no means of ascertaining whether or not anyone else has the subject in hand."

Einhard frankly reveals his motives for writing—his desire to ensure that the "life of this most excellent king" is not "wrapped in the darkness of oblivion" and his gratitude for "the care that King Charles bestowed upon me in my childhood, and my constant friendship with himself and his children after I took up my abode at court."

He concludes with a neat, tactful reaffirmation of his position: "I submit the book. It contains the history of a very great and distinguished man, but there is nothing in it to wonder at besides his deeds"—that is, Einhard is eschewing legendary heroics and sticking to the sober truth—"except the fact that I, who am a barbarian, and very little versed in the Roman language, seem to suppose myself capable of writing gracefully and respectably in Latin . . ."

By our standards, the life lacks development, perspective; yet a clear picture of a mighty individual emerges, and the chief patterns of Charlemagne's character are skillfully detected and revealed—his constancy to his ends, his powers of persuasion, his passion for education. Einhard's biography is far closer to modern biography than his age is to our age, than the rudimentary poetry and drama of his time are to the literary art of our time. In its way, the achievement of the biographer is hardly less to be wondered at than the achievement of the great king.

In briefly touching upon Gregory and Einhard, we are dealing with anomalies, hardy plants which somehow defy the long winter of hagiography. Dominated by the Cleric and the Knight, the Middle Ages reveal how sensitively life-writing answers, how helplessly it submits, to the dominant preoccupations of a time. Whereas it is of the world worldly, the Cleric insisted upon deforming it into an exemplum of other-wordliness, and the Knight found escape from daily brutishness in allegory and chivalric romance and knock-about satire (the *fabliaux*), imaginative expressions alike antithetical to life-writing.

Even the great surge of poetry in fourteenth-century Europe—Dante and Petrarch and Jean de Meung and Chaucer —cannot release biography from its thralldom, though in planting fresh feelings and attitudes, it helps to prepare the escape route. Larger forces are at work too in this century, shaking men's minds into a sharper awareness of the world: the horror of the Black Death, the wasting course of the Hundred Years' War between England and France, the "Captivity" of the Papacy at Avignon and the Great Schism which followed, bloody revolts of peasant and serf, the collapse of the Empire which allows Italian city-states to shape their own destinies.

By the year 1400 the Prince is on his way to the Tower where biography has lain in an enchanted sleep a thousand years.

III

Looking Back:
Biography in the Fifteenth Century—
From Saints to Sinners

W<small>E WESTERN</small> people believe, or used to believe, that certain decisive characteristics of present-day civilization first became vividly discernible in that period of accelerating change to which we gave the name Renaissance.

Today one must almost apologize for using the provocative, or provoking, word.

Renaissance has become a now-you-see-it-now-you-don't period. Numerous historians tell us that the Renaissance never existed, or that if it existed Renaissance is not the right name for it, or that if it did exist and if Renaissance is the right name for it, it did not happen at the time we used to think it happened. We are told that it is just the Middle Ages continuing to evolve; in fact, we are sometimes told that the Middle Ages is more Renaissance than the Renaissance. Or we are informed that it happened in the twelfth century. Or that it happened in the thirteenth century. Or that it happened in Italy perhaps but nowhere else, certainly not in England and in France. Or we are exhorted to believe that what on casual inspection appears to be one Renaissance turns out to be several Renaissances, one inside the other like a nest of tables.

"Renaissance" is of course a metaphor, a rag-bag of concepts; but a rag-bag is better than no container at all. With apologies, then, I will use the term as it was used in more easygoing decades.

Since we recognize in the Renaissance a wonderful efflorescence of literature and art, a heightened awareness of man as a unique and fascinating creature, a surge of curiosity about all things under the heavens, we would reasonably expect to find here the beginnings of modern biography; and, in fact, the sixteenth-century autobiographies of Benvenuto Cellini and Girolamo Cardano and St. Theresa and the semi-autobiographical musings of Montaigne are usually considered, along with a few biographical works like Vasari's *Lives of the Painters* and the *Lives* of Saint Thomas More and Cardinal Wolsey as the heralds of modern life-writing.

But life-writing begins earlier; it begins in Italy and France and England in the fifteenth century, that century which until very recently has been regarded as a literary wasteland, at least in England and France. In this harsh soil the biographical impulse stirs again, after a thousand years in which life-writing had been wrenched from its own orbit to become a captive satellite of the Church.

Indeed, the fifteenth century appears almost as unpropitious as the times of Gregory and Einhard: the last weary spasm of the Middle Ages, an epoch "wandering between two worlds, one dead, the other powerless to be born," a time of dreary endings and abortive beginnings. According to the traditional view, England presents the sorriest spectacle. In history, represented by the dreary clatter of the Wars of the Roses, a tale told by Shakespeare's history plays, full of sound and fury, signifying nothing—but a rousing entertainment at the playhouse. In literature, a desert: the sun of Chaucer has gone down and the crepuscular landscape is lit only be feeble rushlights like Occleve and Lydgate. Caxton grows so bored with it all that he introduces the craft of printing.

We have much the same impression of fifteenth-century France—devastated in the first decades by the English occupation, and dominated in the latter years by the sinister figure of Louis XI, the spider king. François Villon writes dark, wild poetry, of no age and of every age, but it is written in medieval French; and there is Charles d'Orléans, a sort of left-behind troubadour, whose wistful note, if not medieval, perhaps arises from the fact that, taken prisoner at Agincourt, he had to endure twenty-five years of English cooking. In any case, the standard two-volume anthology of Renaissance French literature begins firmly with the reign of Francis I in the early sixteenth century.

Italy would seem to be another story. Italy of the *quattrocento* blazes with the light of humanistic learning, its men of letters and painters and architects and scholars patronized by cultivated tyrants like Francesco Sforza, Duke of Milan, by the famous Houses of Este and Gonzaga, and by Popes thirsty for fame. As far as *belles lettres* is concerned, however, between Petrarch and Boccaccio in the fourteenth century and Lorenzo the Magnificent and Machiavelli a hundred years later, there appears no famous work of imaginative literature.

Yet here in the fifteenth century—in three autobiographies which, neatly enough, represent England, France, and Italy—we shall find the beginnings of the art of modern life-writing, beginnings that anticipate by a century the great burgeoning of literature in sixteenth-century France and Elizabethan England.

In England, until the end of the fourteenth century, the government, the business community, the courts, the towns, kept their records in French or Latin; lords and knights conducted their correspondence in French, when they corresponded at all. Then with amazing suddenness, in a span of less than fifty years during the first decades of the fifteenth century, French well nigh disappeared and Latin faded. The rolls of Parliament, chronicles, letters, town records, were cast in the vernacular. The Englishness of England had arrived. At this same time there developed the impulse not only to enjoy with keener awareness the flavor of living, the drama of character, but also to record these manifestations.

Town records become much fuller and freer; human nature intrudes upon municipal business. The characters and careers of famous mayors are revealed—William Canynges of Bristol, merchant-adventurer extraordinary; bold and enterprising Thomas Wrangwysh of York, friend of Richard III; those almost legendary figures, Simon Eyre and Dick Whittington of London.

The Coventry records offer the life-story of Laurence Saunders, for more than two decades a rebel against the governing oligarchy of the town. His fiery speeches of defiance against a timorous mayor are recorded, the moment in the marketplace when he urges the humble citizens of Coventry to join him in fighting for their liberties, even poems written by his admirers and nailed up on church doors.

For the first time in English history, numbers of letters are now preserved, and they are no longer brief business communications; they thread all the emotional ramifications of domesticity, the bittersweet web of human existence. The Paston letters are too famous to need comment here: they form the autobiography of a tough, intelligent Norfolk clan enmeshed in politics and parental problems, in love and war and death.

But there are other wonderfully revealing collections. The Stonor letters reflect the well-to-do squirearchy, long settled on their land but not above making business alliances and trading in wool; the Plumpton correspondence exposes the turbulent lives of a hard-handed litigious Yorkshire knight and his kindred; the Cely letters embrace a three-cornered exchange carried on by a family of wool merchants from Calais and London and their Essex manor, a gay blade, a black sheep, an ambitious entrepreneur. The Shillingford letters hit off the personality and portray the political struggles of a doughty West Country mayor in the most embattled moments of his life.

In the poetry of the day, otherwise sadly undistinguished, there suddenly appears one pungent autobiographical strain —the *Male Règle* of Thomas Occleve. With wry humor he sings the chancery clerk, sometimes bored and often broke, who was fond of the tavern girls but timid about kissing

them, who splendidly paid his tavern bills without questioning
the total, and who gave far larger tips than he could afford
to the Thames watermen in order to impress on them that he
was a gentleman—an utterly delightful piece that makes one
wish that Occleve had channeled his literary energies into life-
writing.

Out of this milieu, this heightened curiosity about human
behavior and the impulse to record it, comes, in the earlier
half of the century, the first autobiography in English. It
was dictated by Margery Kempe, the sobbing mystic, or
hysteric, of Lynn. Like Julius Caesar in his *Gallic Wars*—
though she certainly did not know Caesar's *Gallic Wars*—she
refers to herself throughout in the third person; but unlike
Caesar, she calls herself, with flamboyant humility, "the creature," that is, the unworthy product of the Creator.

Like Einhard, Margery feels compelled to speak frankly to
the reader. She explains that twenty years had passed after her
first vision before she undertook to record her experience.
Thus it is, she continues, that "this book is not written in
order, each thing after another as it was done, but like as the
matter came to the creature in mind . . ."

Daughter of a mayor of Lynn in Norfolk, she married a
burgess of that town and led, apparently, an ordinary life
until she had her first vision. Then she set forth on her adventures. Unlike other mystics, she bustled about the world,
challenging clerical doctors to fault her orthodoxy, bearding
worldly archbishops, testifying to her illumination by "bois-
terous sobbing" that some considered holy, others wholly
hypocritical, but all found somewhat unnerving. For twenty-
five years she wandered over England, over Europe, made a

pilgrimage to the Holy Land, and then returning to Lynn in her sixties, she began about 1436 to dictate her autobiography.

She was clearly influenced by British and Continental mystics; much of her book is given to the recording of her colloquies with various heavenly powers; and she shows little interest in the exotic places she has visited—Rome, Venice, Jerusalem. Nonetheless, unlike other mystics of her time, Margery was moved by the true biographical impulse: she never permits us to lose sight of the woman, the human being, and the large impact she made upon friend and foe; and she projects her life, artlessly it is true, in a series of vigorous scenes, the mainspring of which is usually dialogue.

Here is Margery brought before the Archbishop of York on suspicion of heresy:

"The archbishop said to her—'I am evil informed of thee. I hear it said that thou art a right wicked woman.'

"And she answered back—'I also hear it said that ye are a wicked man. And if ye be as wicked as men say, ye shall never come to heaven, unless ye amend whilst ye be here.'

"Then he said full boisterously—'Why thou wretch, what say men of me?'

"She answered—'Other men, sir, can tell you well enough.'" In the end, the somewhat harried archbishop paid a servant five shillings to escort her from his diocese with all speed.

Margery was not perhaps without worldly vanity. When the Archbishop first exclaimed, "Where shall I get a man who might lead this woman away from me?"

"Immediately there started up many young men, and every

one of them said—'My lord, I will go with her.'

Margery may have been unbalanced in some ways, but she has the biographer's concern for the truth, picturing very frankly how intensely many folk—from bishops to beggars —disliked her. For example, at Calais, returning from a pilgrimage, she anxiously sought to take ship with some fellow-pilgrims who as anxiously sought to avoid her. She "speered and spied," found out what vessel they had chosen, put her baggage on board—at which they hurriedly trans- ferred to another ship. At the last moment, she managed to join them, leaving her baggage behind.

"The said creature, perceiving by their faces and manner that they had little affection for her person, prayed to Our Lord that He would grant her grace to hold her head up, and preserve her from voiding unclean matter in their presence, so that she would cause them no abomination.

"Her desire was fulfilled, so that, others in the ship voiding and casting full boisterously and uncleanly, she, all of them marvelling, could help them and do what she would."

Thus, flaunting like a flag in the winds of the world both her piety and her personality, Margery Kempe proclaimed the glory of being the creature of the Creator, but she also knew that she was a remarkable woman who had experienced more of life than most folk. Though she announced her pur- pose as being to bring man to God, she could not resist bring- ing Margery Kempe to the reader. Whether she was a mystic or a hysteric, she is a genuine autobiographer.

The second autobiographical manifestation appears in France, a little after the middle of the century. Margery embedded her life, as it were, in a religious tract; the French lord, Jean de Bueil, conceals his in the guise of a romance. The hero after many adventures marries the King's daughter; places are given high-flown fictional names; there are didactic passages designed to teach young men the art of warfare. In fact, the romantic element is but a feeble coloring, probably an attempt to placate popular taste as well as to cover the author's nakedness in an age unaccustomed to self-revelation. The heart of *Le Jouvencel—The Youngster*—is autobiographical.

Jean de Bueil, beginning his career in the grim Anglo-French war of the early fifteenth century as a man of arms, a gentleman of the cavalry, rose with the rising fortunes of France to become one of the chief generals, and then Admiral, of the realm. In his old age he dictated *The Youngster* to three of his servants. Though he hides his personality and the actual events of his career behind his nameless hero, he nevertheless endows that character with his own experience of existence. He seeks to reveal why a young man can find in the profession of arms a worthwhile life even as he depicts realistically the miserable, weary, brutish warfare of ambush and pillage—not the sweep of great campaigns but incessant skirmishes between small bands garrisoned in neighboring castles, a war of sallies and raids and humble exploits.

To show you how far Bueil's world is from the world of *Sir Gawain and the Green Knight*—the youngster begins his career by capturing goats from a neighboring fortress. He then carries off laundry from which he makes himself a padded military coat called a jack. He progresses to the point of capturing the enemy captain's cow, and soon he is taking part in a successful ambush. Having proved himself a promising young warrior and won a breastplate and horse for himself, he then learns to lead a small body of troops, and finally he becomes a commander of armies.

Crude though the narrative is, it succeeds in its best moments in recapturing a life being lived—a fledgling soldier riding the roads at night, ears strained for sounds betokening the approach of the enemy; the emotions of the youngster going into combat with his companions: "a great sweet feeling of loyalty and pity fills your heart upon seeing your friend so valiantly exposing his body. . . . And then you prepare to go and die or live with him, and for love not to abandon him . . ."

For all their obvious deficiencies as artists, Margery Kempe and Jean de Bueil speak with a fresh voice, grapple with the stuff of human experience. Though their autobiographies are encrusted with unbiographical matter—the medieval age still retaining its grip—they signal the dawn of modern lifewriting.

A year or two before Bueil dictated *Le Jouvencel*, a famous Italian completed his autobiography, writing the last of it just a few months before his death.

There was a good deal of biographical activity in fifteenth century Italy, but only this one autobiographical exemplar of true biography. The sketches of famous Florentines by Villani, for instance, are of limited scope; and the biographies of prince-patrons produced by humanists—like Simonetta's Life of Francesco Sforza and Panormita's Alphonsus of Aragon—turn out to be mere panegyrics.

The exception is the autobiography—misleadingly titled *The Commentaries*—of Aeneas Sylvius Piccolomini, who composed the work after he became Pope Pius II, the only Pope to set his hand to this form of self-revelation. Aeneas, one of the humanistic luminaries of the Renaissance, takes us into another world from that of Margery Kempe and Jean de Bueil. He produces a highly self-conscious, richly developed work of art.

It is by any standard an astonishing piece of literature, and no less astonishing is the neglect that it has suffered—except as an historical document, mere source-material. Not until recent years was it translated from the Latin and edited, in exemplary fashion, by two Smith College professors; unfortunately, their edition is scattered through several issues of the *Smith College Bulletin*, and a paperback reprint, titled *Memoirs of a Renaissance Pope*, is sadly abridged. It has been generally ignored by writers on autobiography—Roy Pascal's excellent *Design and Truth in Autobiography*, for example, has a good deal to say about Petrarch's brief *Letter to Posterity* but does not mention Pius' large-scale work, though the latter offers a most unusual autobiographical design. Indeed, this obscure fifteenth-century autobiography stands comparison with the autobiographies the world has most acclaimed—a brilliant life brilliantly recounted by the man who lived it.

In this first age of modern political adventurers—Warwick the Kingmaker; Don Juan Pacheco in Castile; Francesco Sforza, the bastard son of a free-lance soldier who made himself Duke of Milan—Aeneas Sylvius Piccolomini adventured, in his way, with the boldest of them, using his learning and his eloquence to carve out a career. After studying at the University of Siena, he made himself variously useful as diplomat, propagandist, counsellor. He served the Council of Bâle against the papacy. He was secretary to two Popes, an Anti-Pope, and the Emperor, Frederick III. At first-hand, he knew Europe from Scotland to the Balkans. He wrote novels and poems, composed a history of Bohemia and works on geography, issued pamphlets on education and on horse-breeding. The Emperor crowned him poet-laureate. Then, well into middle age, this "condottiere of letters" took Holy Orders; after a meteoric rise in the Church he was elected Pope in 1458 at the age of fifty-three.

It is then that he began to compose his autobiography, which in imitation of Caesar he called *Commentaries*. Like Caesar (and Margery Kempe and Jean de Bueil) he wrote in the third person. In Book One of the work he gives an account of his career up to his elevation to the papacy; the succeeding eleven books and a fragment of a twelfth, which breaks off only a few months before his death in 1464, depict the life of the Pope.

Nothing is more remarkable about this remarkable production than its apparently obvious yet subtle and complex viewpoint. The Caesarian third-person clearly satisfied his humanist taste, but it was not imposed as an arbitrary convention; it grows out of his own nature, a design which reveals as well as frames his personality.

Aeneas accepted without question the articles and the practice of the Faith; there was too much blood in him for religious ardor and soul-searching; his trained intelligence looked askance at miracle-mongering (except when it served to propagate his cherished design of a Crusade). Neither as cleric nor as artist was he introspective: he is thoroughly immersed in the world and the eyes of his spirit turn outward.

He is, furthermore, as his career as well as the *Commentaries* show, the playmaker of his drama: he watches himself acting out his life. Thus the third person expresses, in art, the true duality of his nature. "He," the watcher, writes of "I," the watched, Aeneas, the man of letters, bending his talents to portray that fascinating being, the triple-tiaraed emperor of Christendom.

No less noteworthy than the relation between the life-writer and the life is the relationship between the life-writer and the life-considered-as-literary-material. Only the first book is written from that distance of memory which establishes the tone of true autobiography; the remaining books come into being even as the life-material does. Yet Aeneas, writing (or dictating) at irregular intervals, shedding the weight of the papacy in the lateness of night, avoids the diurnal atmosphere of the diary entry and, consciously or unconsciously, achieves the perspective of retrospection. The shortened memory-distance enlarges the scope and magnifies the details of the autobiographical panorama but it is not permitted to impose the artless immediacy of journal or diary.

Not only does Aeneas thus create a special perspective as regards himself as writer and his material, but he likewise creates a special—or false or artful—perspective in the other direction, as regards his material and the reader. With disarming frankness, he addresses himself confidently to posterity:

"Why then do we so strive for the glory of a fair name? Let the argumentative think what they please about the dead, provided they do not deny that while men live they take pleasure in the glory of the present, which they hope will continue after death. It is this which sustains the most brilliant

intellects and even more than the hope of a celestial life. . . .
After his death envy will be still, and when those passions
which warp the judgement are no more, true report will rise
again and number Pius among the illustrious popes."

More than a gesture of rhetoric, this address to posterity
heralds a self-conscious establishment of distance between the
material and the reader. Aeneas describes places, customs,
ceremonies, as if he were a man from a later age recreating a
background no longer familiar; likewise the portraits he
draws of some of his bizarre contemporaries have the air of
explaining his milieu to a future audience rather than of
simply reporting it as the texture of his experience. Aeneas
assumes a middle distance between his material on the one
hand and his reader on the other, pushing each of them
farther away from himself than mere actuality would dictate.

These facets of his complex viewpoint combine to create
for the third-person narrative a dignity, an authenticity,
which transcend device—whereas, for example, its employ-
ment by Henry Adams in *The Education* lies somewhat
eccentrically athwart a fabric so mental, so inward. The *Commentaries* are thus the most *biographical* of the great autobiographies, even though they are among the most exuberantly
self-celebrating. It is almost as if they were composed by a
bosom friend or secretary who shared Pope Pius' illusions
as well as his secrets. We may well suppose that the viewpoint
serves as a release, and a graceful excuse, for the exuberance.

Paradoxically enough, Aeneas' enjoyment of himself is so
secure that it serves rather to stimulate than to limit frankness;
and Aeneas the author, for all his admiration for his subject,
breaks through the reticenes of Piccolomini the Pope. Despite

the dam of vanity and circumspection, trust keeps flooding in.

Aeneas zestfully recreates the world-scene in which the Pope exerts his powers—a panorama of kings and princes whom he castigated or cajoled, Italian robber-barons, cynical condottieri, monks and madmen, strangely clad delegations come from far reaches of the earth. He likewise takes us into the Vatican where, behind closed doors, the Pope berates or manipulates his Cardinals, using all the political tricks in his extensive repertory, and comments with acerbity (but without anguish) on the ostentatious profligacies of some of his Cardinals, particularly those whom he dislikes.

After a lifetime of making his way in the world, he had little Christian charity left for the great figures, or the peoples, of that world. He sees himself as a master-intelligence beleaguered by universal corruption and stupidity; and his comments on mankind grow increasingly acidulous as he vainly struggles to reanimate the papacy by one grand stroke, a Crusade against the Turks.

The Germans are barbarians. The French, intolerably conceited, are a parcel of fools ruled by a fool (Louis XI, whom the Pope succeeds in deceiving just once, to his own cost). Lest he be thought to exhibit Italian prejudice, Aeneas makes clear that the Italians, if brainier, are even more corrupt. The Venetians are summed up as soulless money-grubbers, and the Florentines are not appreciably better. Though he grudgingly admits that Cosimo de Medici is an astute politician "who knows everything that goes on in Italy" and that he is "more cultured than most merchants," he finds Cosimo deceitful and avaricious.

As for the princes of Italy, except for Francesco Sforza, his fellow-adventurer, and Federigo of Urbino, who, being "well read," was able to follow the Pope's conversation when he spoke of Homeric military strategy, they are violent, treacherous, Church-hating. With undisguised relish, Aeneas applies himself to portray that epitome of the Renaissance tyrant, Sigismundo Malatesta, Lord of Rimini. As cultured as cruel, Sigismundo, Aeneas admits, was "very vigorous in body and mind, eloquent, and gifted with great military ability. He had a thorough knowledge of history and no slight acquaintance with philosophy." But "his lust was so unbridled that he violated his daughters and his sons-in-law. When he was a lad, he often played the bride and after taking the woman's part debauched men. No marriage was sacred to him. He ravished nuns and outraged Jewesses; boys and girls who would not submit to him he had murdered or savagely beaten. . . . Of all men who have ever lived or ever will live he was the worst scoundrel, the disgrace of Italy and the infamy of our times." He also happened to be at war with the armies of the Church. Aeneas records how that master propagandist, the Pope, put the quietus on Sigismundo. For this purpose, Pius staged an anti-canonization, in which with approporiate maledictions Sigismundo was officially consigned to hell and then publicly burned in effigy.

Pius II loved to cut a fine figure in the world, and he had no doubt of the enormous eminence of the papal throne. Yet Aeneas the biographer, innocent of dignity, cannot resist laying bare all manner of bizarre truths and racy goings-on. He even dares to violate that secret of secrets, the consistory of Cardinals electing a Pope, in order to reveal the means by which he secured the Tiara.

On the first "scrutiny" the Cardinal of Siena (our hero) and the Cardinal of Bologna lead with five votes apiece. Then begins a fierce bargaining, with supporters of the French Cardinal of Rouen gaining strength. Finally the Cardinals retire to bed. Suddenly, "some time after midnight" a friend wakes Aeneas with the news that Rouen's backers are meeting secretly in the privies—"a fit place for such a Pope to be elected!" Aeneas observes—in order to cinch the election and divide the spoils of office.

By dawn Aeneas is working feverishly on Cardinal after Cardinal. "You will find youself among the hindmost, if a Frenchman is Pope; take care, you fool!" he tells one. He warns another, "You will find the College [of Cardinals] filled with Frenchmen!" Thus he threatens, pleads with, overwhelms with persuasions the yet uncommitted Cardinals. Then comes the morning scrutiny. Rouen is one of the three cardinals assigned to watch the golden chalice in which one by one the cardinals cast their ballots.

"When Aeneas came up to put in his ballot, Rouen, pale and trembling, said 'Look, Aeneas! I commend myself to you' —certainly a rash thing to say when it was not allowable to change what he had written. But ambition overcame prudence. Aeneas said, 'Do you commend yourself to a worm like me?' And without another word he dropped his ballot in the cup and went back to his place." When the ballots are counted, Rouen announces that Aeneas has eight votes. But our hero "did not allow himself to be defrauded,' popping up at once with "'Look more carefully at the ballots for I have nine votes.'"

Twelve votes were needed for election, and so the Cardinals entered on the period of "accession," or open changing of votes.

For some time no one spoke, no one opened his lips, no one moved any part of his body except the eyes, which kept glancing all about. It was a strange silence and a strange sight, men sitting there like their own statues; no sound to be heard, no movement to be seen. They remained thus for some moments, those inferior in rank waiting for their superiors to begin the accession.

Then Rodrigo, the Vice-Chancellor [later the notorious Pope Alexander VI], rose and said, "I accede to the Cardinal of Siena," an utterance which was like a dagger in Rouen's heart, so pale did he turn. A silence followed and each man looking at his neighbor, began to indicate his sentiments by gestures. By this time it looked as if Aeneas would be pope and some, fearing this result, left the conclave, pretending physical needs, but really with the purpose of escaping the fate of that day. Those who thus withdrew were the Cardinals of Ruthen and San Sisto. However, as no one followed them, they soon returned. Then Jacopo, Cardinal of Sant' Anastasia, said, "I accede to the Cardinal of Siena." At this all appeared even more stunned, like people in a house shaken by unprecedented earthquakes, and lost the power of speech.

Aeneas now lacked but one vote, for twelve would elect a pope. Realizing this, Cardinal Prospero Colonna thought that he must get for himself the glory of announcing the pope. He rose and was about to pronounce his vote with the customary dignity, when he was seized by the Cardinals of Nicaea and Rouen and sharply rebuked for wishing to accede to Aeneas. When he persisted in his intention, they tried to get him out of the room by force, resorting even to such means to snatch the papacy from Aeneas. But Prospero,

who, though he had voted for the Cardinal of Rouen on his
ballot, was nevertheless bound to Aeneas by ties of old friendship, paid no attention to their abuse and empty threats.
Turning to the other cardinals, he said, "I too accede to the
Cardinal of Siena and I make him pope." When they heard
this, the courage of the opposition failed and all their mach-
inations were shattered.

All the cardinals immediately fell at Aeneas's feet and saluted him as Pope.

Aeneas blandly records that he then informed the Cardinals, "What is done by two-thirds of the Sacred College is
surely of the Holy Ghost, which may not be resisted."

Nor does our autobiographer hesitate to show himself, as
Pope, in postures which are hardly consonant with the aura of
the Holy Office. On one occasion, he brusquely refused certain church benefices to the French Cardinal of Arras, whom
he loathed—"a courtesan of Tivoli who had slept with him
said she had lain with a wineskin." "Then Arras had recourse
to Gallic wiles. He promised the Pope 12,000 ducats if he got
what he wanted. The Pope burst out furiously, 'Go to the
devil, you and your threats! and your money go to hell with
you!'"

But I have still not touched on one of the most remarkable
psychological manifestations of this autobiography. Our hero
sees himself not only as a force, a pyrotechnical display of
humanity in action, but also as sensibility. He is more than
Pope, he is poet-Pope; and Aeneas is always eager to demonstrate with what *flair* the enlightened heir of classical civilization within the robes of the Pontiff combines his Office and
his cultivation. He pictures himself as a tourist of taste, a
connoisseur of natural beauties, a sensitive investigator of

antiquities.

On one of his holiday journeys, humble folk stage a boat-race for his pleasure. The Pope finds himself enmeshed in business, but, he is careful to record, he breaks off now and then to watch the race—as befits the many-sided gentleman. Tivoli, with its magnificent landscapes and the ruin of Hadrian's villa, is one of his favorite haunts; he romantically responds to craggy mountains and olive groves and temples ruined by time with a bravura reminiscent of Byron's *Childe Harold*, Cantos three and four.

"All about Tivoli in summer are the most delightful green fields where the pope used often to go with the cardinals for refreshment of mind, sometimes sitting in a grassy nook under the olives, sometimes in a green meadow on the edge of the river Aniene where they could look down into the translucent water. . . . Pius often rested in these meadows by bubbling springs or under the shade of trees, talking with the cardinals about state matters or hearing the embassies which followed him wherever he went."

Yet in the wildest places he is always a man of the world. He enthusiastically describes a great garden made by monks who live on a mountaintop—"There are groves of cypress trees where in summer one may find pleasant shade. Vineyards too and leafy vines and vegetable gardens and swimming pools and an unfailing spring and cisterns and wells, and on the cliffs themselves oak forests and juniper. Many paths wide enough for two men wind round the hill and cut it in two. They are planted on both sides with vines and rosebuds or rosemary, delightful refreshment for the monks—and even more delightful for those who are at liberty to depart after seeing them."

Aeneas depicts himself amidst these scenes so self-consciously that he is like a stage manager arranging a set. Indeed, it is impossible not to suspect that Aeneas arranged his picnics, stationed himself by the waterfall at Tivoli, posed beside a Roman ruin, with at least some thought that he could record the scene afterwards. Thus he resembles that master of the biographical art, James Boswell, who deliberately created moments in Samuel Johnson's life—as when he arranged for Johnson to meet Wilkes—so that he might use them in his biography. This is the ultimate plasticity of biographical resources, the rare moment when the biographer can, in advance, adjust his materials to his needs.

Like Einhard, like Margery Kempe, Aeneas feels obligated to affirm his biographical good faith: "You who are to read . . . must understand that we have kept the law of history, not to depart from the truth."

Pius II is probably justly regarded as not one of the greatest popes, though one of the most remarkable; but Aeneas Sylvius Piccolomini has been unjustly neglected as the author of an autobiography which must be ranked among the half-dozen greatest of its kind.

We turn now from the three autobiographies heralding modern life-writing, to three biographies, one French and two English, which, like Pius' *Commentaries*, represent an extraordinary biographical accomplishment, an unexpected efflorescence, in the very dawn of our era—and a promise that, in the subsequent development of English biography, will not be fulfilled.

The *Memoirs* of Philippe de Commynes, written at the end of the fifteenth century, have long been praised for their limpid prose, sagacious observations, and historical—and political—usefulness. The Emperor Charles V called them "a textbook for princes"; for they reveal the successful practice of the *realpolitik* which Machiavelli a little later in *The Prince* adumbrated in theory. Montaigne admired the style both of the *Memoirs* and of the mind that conceived them; they are "lit by the obvious good faith of the author" who is "exempt from vanity in speaking of himself and from prejudice and envy speaking of others."

Unlike Pius II, Philippe de Commynes was not a humanist —he deplores the fact that he was trained in arms rather than in learning—though he made himself into a well-educated man, particularly in history. Thus he represents not the classical surge of the Renaissance but the native enlargement of awareness, the quickening flexibility of mind, in Western Europe which the revival of the classics would but spur and accelerate. How this young squire, reared like so many young squires of his day and, typically, entering the service of his prince, managed to free himself from medieval habits of thinking and feeling and achieve so balanced, clear-sighted, and penetrating a view of men and affairs remains a mystery of genetics-environment, and of will. Commynes senses deeply the hand of God within the world, but he is alert to human causes-and-effects and he firmly believes, like men of the coming age, in the plasticity of human development, man's capacity to master large areas of his destiny by intelligence and will. In numerous digressions he is at pains to emphasize the implicit moral revelation of the *Memoirs*, that stupidity and indifference are the great sins, that through education and the willed use of the mind the rulers of men can avoid, for themselves and their subjects, the miseries of disaster or failure which they foolishly ascribe to fortune. He despises brutality, violence, empty gestures of pomp, blind ambition; and in his writing and his career he steadily upholds the way of peace and the values of assiduity, a trained awareness, the capacity to recognize good counsel.

This invigorating moral texture develops organically from the stuff of Commynes' book, which turns out to be something other than it appears. It is as memoirs that the work has been widely celebrated: that form of autobiography in which the writer relates the subtance of his experience—what *me* has learned about the *not-me*—rather than unfolds the operation of its effects on himself and his life; in this case, an historical commentary and a political handbook by a man in the thick of great affairs. Yet, though Commynes puts himself into his work, the first two-thirds of the *Memoirs* are, in reality, a biography of King Louis XI of France, and even the last part—apparently pure memoirs, for Commynes continues the relation of his career after the death of Louis—is subtly encompassed within the biographical frame, as we shall see. Like the *Apology* of Plato, like Boswell's *Johnson*, the *Memoirs* spring from the life-relationship of two most remarkable beings, a rare conjunction of the shrewdest counsellor of the age and its grand wizard of statecraft.

The biography is thematically developed by means of pervasive contrast. The reign of Louis XI was shaped by a mortal conflict which tested all his talents and exposed all the facets of his quicksilver personality. Bending his faculties to transform a loose-knit feudal realm into a national state, Louis came into violent collision with his greatest vassal, Charles the Rash, Duke of Burgundy, whose ardent brain held but two purposes, to smash the rising power of France and carve out for himself a mighty kingdom stretching from the North Sea to the Alps.

Commynes brilliantly sets off the indefatigable concentration, the marvelous humor and the deadly patience, the mastery of diplomatic maneuver, the preternatural insight into human motives of Louis XI, who, despising the waste and the crude fortuities of warfare, put his faith in intelligence, against the glory-hungry Charles of Burgundy, heedless of all counsel except his own ambitions, who furiously plunged into a career of war. That Commynes does not disguise the spectacular failures and impulsive errors of King Louis serves only to emphasize the quality of his triumph, when, finally, the network of economic and political diplomacy Louis inexorably kept weaving—he is the inventor of Cold War—crushed the dream and the life of the Duke of Burgundy.

There was no man in the world so suited to record the life of this king as Philippe de Commynes: for eight years he served as counsellor to the roaring lion, and then one night, in the summer of 1472, he stole from the Burgundian camp to become the most intimate adviser of the fox, and his biographer.

Though, in life, Commynes exercises all the sober responsibility and unshakable prudence of the professional man of state, he proves in his *Memoirs* to have been endowed with a superb appreciation of those high moments in which character most vividly displays itself. Again and again the biography, sensitively responding to the dramatic rhythms of King Louis' life, gathers its forces and rises into a great scene: Louis at Péronne, in 1468, delivered by his own gambler's instinct into the hands of an infuriated Duke of Burgundy; Louis skillfully buying off Edward IV's invasion of 1475 and, all charm, meeting Edward on the bridge at Picquigny; Louis, early in 1477, getting word of the crown of his labors, the destruction of Charles the Rash—a varied procession of dramatic moments which unmistakably confirm the *Memoirs* as a work of biographical artistry.

There is a "screen scene" worthy of high comedy, conceived and enacted by Louis in the hope of inflaming his enemy Charles of Burgundy against another enemy of his, the Count of St. Pol, supposedly faithful to Charles. Stationing a captured Burgundian lord behind a fire-screen, Louis receives an envoy of St. Pol and dexterously encourages him to deride the Duke of Burgundy. Speak up! Louis cries, as the envoy begins to mimic the Duke, I'm getting a little deaf! Not long after, Duke Charles delivered St. Pol into Louis' hands.

Even the most famous of these scenes, Louis' adventures at Péronne and at Picquigny, do not exceed the culminating moment of the biography proper, the powerfully moving deathbed of a king who terribly feared death, as compassionately witnessed by Commynes himself.

The concluding portion of the *Memoirs* which continue the affairs of France and Commynes' part in them, can be seen as an epilogue to the biography, a coda which, like the biography itself, employs patterns of contrast and thus creates a commentary on the life of Louis XI.

The first contrast springs from the altered standpoint of the biographer himself—formerly the trusted agent of Louis, a king who knew how to listen to and act upon good advice, and now, in the reign of Louis' son Charles VIII, a voice unheeded, his diplomacy hamstrung and his counsel disregarded because of Charles' indifference and the enmity of the second-raters who have won the new king's ear. The second contrast turns on policy. Louis XI, sagaciously refusing to seek power in Italy by armed intervention, had by his statecraft become the virtual overlord of the Italian states, the benevolent patron of the Italian Renaissance; whereas feckless Charles VIII, pushed by his favorites, undertook the famous invasion of Italy of 1494 which barely skirted disaster and ended in waste and failure. Finally, Commynes deepens our appreciation of the endlessly diligent, witty, subtle father in presenting the portrait of his mediocre and pleasure-loving son, the ruler who does not understand his business and allows himself to be manipulated by others.

Thus, in consequence of this second master-pattern of contrast, King Louis XI, like Hamlet offstage, remains constantly in our minds. The last portion of the *Memoirs*, seemingly unbiographical, actually completes the picture of Louis' character and achievement.

At the conclusion Commynes puts himself in the scene to sign his name, as it were, and so authenticate the work. Two days after the death of Charles VIII, he arrives at Amboise to pray beside the body. He narrates Charles' last hours, "for though I was indeed not present, his confessor and his most intimate chamberlains recounted them to me." The careless king had died carelessly. As he entered a broken-down gallery to watch a game of tennis, he bumped his head on a doorframe. This apparently slight accident threw him into convulsions. He spent his last moments "stretched on a rude pile of straw in a mean building which stank because people used it as a place to urinate."

This passage reveals yet another remarkable facet of Commynes' literary powers. To his firmly conceived moral perspective and biographical stance Commynes adds the dimension of irony to complete the artful establishment of viewpoint. This ironic detachment, *sec* yet pungent, saturates the *Memoirs*. Sometimes it takes the form of witty comment, as when he observes of a Frenchman and a Burgundian fleeing in opposite directions from the battle of Montlhéry, "Those two were not eager to murder each other." Often Commynes simply juxtaposes illusions and actuality, the gesture and the fact, without comment, or widens his aperture to show absurdities grinning at the edges of pomposity or pretense, or, poker-faced, undermines appearances by understatement.

This pervasive irony crowns an amazing biographical performance: not until the twentieth century will biographers again fully achieve the effects of ironic detachment developed by Commynes at the end of the fifteenth.

Like Einhard, like Pius II, Commynes feels impelled to offer his credentials to the reader, and enter into an engagement to tell the truth:

> Of his youth [that is, the youth of Louis XI] I cannot speak, except from hearsay; but from the time I entered his service until the hour of his death, at which I was present, I have been more continually at his side and engaged in his great affairs than any other man of my rank. It may be that

occasionally in this writing there will be found something that does not redound to his praise, because I refuse to tell any lies. Nevertheless I do not believe I have ever known a prince in whom there were so few vices as in him, and I have had as considerable an acquaintance with great princes as any man who has lived in France in my time.

Commynes is the earliest, and remains the greatest, biographer of Louis XI: the first masterpiece of biography in the modern world recaptures a master-statesman who helped to shape that world.

We turn, finally, to the first two genuine biographies written in England, and in English, Roper's *Life* of Thomas More and Cavendish's *Wolsey*. Though they did not come into being until the mid-sixteenth century, I think it can be shown that they represent a culmination, not a beginning, that they spring from the progressive interaction of changing native attitudes and international humanism which developed in the fifteenth century.

The new learning made its way into fifteenth-century England slowly, as an exotic. A few clerics betook themselves to Italy in order to study at Padua or Bologna; others who remained at home corresponded with scholars and amassed manuscripts. Three noblemen conspicuously anticipated the currents of time in their patronage and practice of literature: Duke Humphrey of Gloucester (died 1447), younger brother of Henry V, famous for his library; John Tiptoft, Earl of Worcester (died 1470), the first "Italianate Englishman," translator of Cicero; and Anthony Woodville, Earl Rivers (died 1483), whose translation, *The*

Dictes and Sayings of the Philosophers, was one of the first books published by Caxton. Worcester and Rivers, along with humanist prelates like Warwick the Kingmaker's brother, George Neville, Archbishop of York, and Bishop John Sherwood of Durham and John Gunthorpe, Dean of Wells, served Edward IV as diplomats and councillors and brought a new sophistication of learning to the Yorkist Court. This imported humanism makes its biographical mark in the Latin *Life of Henry V* of Tito Livio, which was commissioned by Humphrey of Gloucester, and the much inferior Latin *Life of Henry VII* composed by Henry's court-humanist, Bernard André.

By the time Henry VIII's reign opens in 1509, humanism has melded into the native intellectual scene to produce the heady atmosphere in which Thomas More, John Colet, and Erasmus flourished. This second stage in the domestication of the new learning is biographically signaled by More's *History of Richard III*, written about 1513 in both an English and a Latin version.

The creative exuberance, the self-conscious use of language as an esthetic instrument, the obvious but happy rhythms of More's sinuous sentences establish the *History* as the first exemplar of modern English prose. Richard III, he informs us with relish, "was close and secret, a deep dissembler, lowly of countenance, arrogant of heart, outwardly companionable where he inwardly hated, not hesitating to kiss whom he thought to kill . . ." When he describes Jane Shore, the famous mistress of Edward IV, the tonal effect delicately suggests his compassion: "Proper she was and fair; nothing in her body that you would have changed, unless you would have wished her somewhat higher. Thus say they that knew her in her youth. Albeit some that now see her (for yet she lives) deem her never to have been well visaged. Whose judgement seems to me somewhat like as though men should guess the beauty of one long before departed by her scalp taken out of the charnel house . . ."

More's wit and irony are laid on with a trowel as compared with Commynes' but perfectly suit the high colors of his style. On recording Richard's malicious determination to make Jane Shore undergo a public degradation, More comments, "And for this reason (as a goodly continent Prince, clean and faultless of himself, sent out of heaven into this vicious world for the amendment of men's manners) he caused the Bishop of London to put her to open penance . . ." Like Commynes too, Thomas More had a highly developed sense of drama, and unfolds his *History* by a series of vivid scenes, the most famous of which Shakespeare followed closely in his *Richard III:* that council-meeting in the Tower at which dissembling Richard, before he pounces on Lord Hastings, casually asks the Bishop of Ely to send out for a mess of strawberries.

Unfortunately, the *History of Richard III* is not an achieved biography. In the first place, it is unfinished, breaking off in the midst of one of its most brilliantly ironic scenes (the wily Bishop of Ely entrammeling his jailor, the Duke of Buckingham, in a plot against King Richard). More important, the *History* cannot meet, and probably was not intended to meet, the prime test of biographical writing, truth. Under the influence of classical and humanist historians, More works up great swatches of dialogue—comprising a third of the book—which are wonderfully eloquent but not recorded from life. Furthermore, he fashions the portrait, not of a man but of a monster, that crook-backed demon appropriated by the youthful Shakespeare to make a bustling, melodramatic tragedy.

It is not only that Thomas More received biased information from deadly enemies of Richard like Archbishop Morton (the erstwhile Bishop of Ely). It appears that More was seeking to shape a horrible example, a humanist warning to the ambitious rulers of his day; indeed, he endows Richard with those dark powers of dissimulation which he heartily disliked in Richard's vanquisher, Henry VII—and it may be that he abandoned his work out of prudence or frustration, since Henry himself was just about to appear in it. In any case, both the quality of his sources and his purpose prevented him from creating a true biography. The *History* is a halfway house between the "imported" *Life of Henry V* and the biographical fulfillment of fifteenth-century awakenings for which More's own life would provide material.

Neither More's son-in-law, William Roper, nor the gentleman-usher of Cardinal Wolsey, George Cavendish, was even remotely a humanist; but the biographies they composed spring from English life of the first half of the sixteenth century which had been pervasively quickened by the forces of humanism.

Until recently, however, these books, quite neglected, have been cursorily dismissed as hangers-on from the past, Roper's work representing the medieval saint's life and Cavendish's, the medieval pattern of "tragedie," man rising to greatness and falling to ignominy upon Fortune's Wheel. C. S. Lewis, for example, in his *English Literature in the Sixteenth Century*, devotes only four pages to More's *History*, Roper, and Cavendish together, and firmly disposes of Cavendish thus— "This is perhaps the last work written in English which belongs completely to the Middle Ages."

It would be hard to find a less inspired literary judgment. It is true that, since Thomas More has been canonized, Roper's book may be called a saint's life; and it is true that Cavendish interrupts his work to exclaim against the "inconstant mutability of the uncertain world" (but so did Spenser and the Elizabethan *Mirror for Magistrates*), and in the end cries, "Oh what inconstant trust and assurance is in rolling fortune!" However, we have but to glance at a page of Roper or Cavendish, then recall medieval hagiography and medieval allegorizing, the level of medieval awareness and the limits of the medieval view of man, to realize at once that the evocations of personality shaped into the unfolding of a life which Roper and Cavendish achieve are as unmedieval, as organically an issue of the new age, as the poetry of Wyatt and Surrey, the prose of More.

Furthermore, the great *theme* of both these biographies—in contrast to "medieval" *phrasings* that Marlowe and Shakespeare and Raleigh would also use—grows out of the particular political milieu in which Thomas More and Thomas Wolsey lived and in which Roper and Cavendish observed them living. That theme is the relationship between king and subject, especially subject-as-counsellor, a relationship pregnant with hideous dangers as the result of the semi-absolutist rule fastened upon England by that brutal political genius, that bluff and terrible master, Henry VIII. The theme is a Renaissance byword: *Indignatio principis mors est*—the Prince's anger is fatal.

This theme does not lie implicit in the material but is developed with conscious irony by both biographers as a shaping principle of their books. The anger of the prince is fatal to Wolsey, yet turns him from an arrogant prelate, raised high above mankind, into a fallible human being whom we can sympathetically understand and who in his final sufferings even begins to understand himself; and the anger of the Prince is fatal to Thomas More, but only to his body, for in remaining true to himself he shows the theme as an ironic delusion.

Roper's *Life* of his father-in-law is more limited—there is no mention of Erasmus or even of the writing of *Utopia*—and not so delicately designed as Cavendish's *Life* of Wolsey, but it is a work of deliberate art, nonetheless. In a series of intimate scenes, Roper develops the struggle within Thomas More between his duty to his conscience and his duty to his king, between his love of life and his love of truth, these scenes moving toward their climax as More leaves his house and family in Chelsea for the last time:

"And whereas he evermore used before at his departure from his wife and children, whom he tenderly loved, to have them bring him to his boat, and there to kiss them all and bid them farewell; then [at this moment] would he suffer none of them forth of the gate to follow him, but pulled the wicket after him and shut them all from him. And with an heavy heart, as by his countenance it appeared, with me and our four servants there took he his boat towards Lambeth [where he was to be examined by the King's commissioners].

Wherein sitting still sadly a while, at last he suddenly whispered me in the ear and said 'Son Roper, I thank our Lord the field is won.' "

After More has been committed to the Tower, Roper presents an interview between Sir Thomas and his wife Alice, a woman who had little understanding of her husband—surely one of the greatest scenes in biographical literature:

"What the good-year, master More, quoth she, I marvel that you that have always hitherto been taken for so wise a man will now so play the fool to lie here in this close, filthy prison . . . when . . . you have at Chelsea a right fair house, your library, your books, your gallery, your gardens . . . the company of me your wife, your children, and household. . . .

"After he had a while quietly heard her, with a cheerful countenance he said unto her: I pray thee, good mistress Alice, tell me one thing.

"What is that? quoth she.

"Is not this house, quoth he, as nigh heaven as my own?

"To whom she, after her accustomed homely fashion, not liking such talk, answered: Tilly-vale, tilly-vale!

"How say you, mistress Alice, quoth he, is it not so?

"Bone deus, bone deus, man, will this gear never be left? quoth she."

And there, to the very marrow of life, are Sir Thomas More and his spouse—More with his marvelous grace under pressure; Alice representing the misunderstanding of the world as well as the wife whose lack of communion with himself he cheerfully bears.

Within this dramatic pattern Roper develops his informing ironic theme. Early in the biography, revealing the "entire favor" that Henry VIII bore to Sir Thomas, Roper recounts a scene between More and the King. "And for the pleasure he [Henry VIII] took in his company would His Grace suddenly sometime come home to his house at Chelsea to be merry with him; and after dinner, in a fair garden of his, walked with him by the space of an hour, holding his arm about his neck.

"As soon as His Grace was gone, I, rejoicing thereat, told Sir Thomas More how happy he was, whom the King had so familiarly entertained, as I never had seen him do to any other except Cardinal Wolsey, whom I saw His Grace once walk with, arm in arm. I thank our Lord, son, quoth he, I find his grace my very good Lord indeed; and I believe he doth singularly favor me as any subject within this realm. Howbeit, son Roper, I may tell thee I have no cause to be proud thereof, for if my head could win him a castle in France . . . it should not fail to go."

Then at the very end, after the poignantly terse account of More's execution, Roper suddenly shifts us overseas, to the court of the Emperor. When Charles V learns of More's death from the English ambassador, Sir Thomas Elyot, he exclaims, "This will we say, that if we had been the master of such a servant, of whose doings ourself have had these many years no small experience, we would rather have lost the best city of our dominions than have lost such a worthy counsellor.

"Which matter," Roper finishes, signing his name as biographical warranty to the work, "was by the same Sir Thomas Elyot to myself reported." Between these ironically juxtaposed scenes are staged the life and death of Sir Thomas More.

Just as Roper controls his material not only by thematic and dramatic patterns but also by maintaining a decisive point of view—that of the unwitting son-in-law become the confidant of greatness—so too does George Cavendish rigorously order his subject-matter by his biographical stance. He unfolds the life of Cardinal Wolsey from the viewpoint of an intimate servant, Wolsey's gentleman usher, the arranger of occasions and ceremonies, as he himself actually observed and shared it. Cavendish's work is considerably longer, more richly developed, more tightly shaped than Roper's. Almost exactly half the biography portrays the rise and the glory of the great cardinal, the narrative dwelling on themes of pompous splendor, as befits the viewpoint of the narrator. The last half depicts the fallen minister, struck down by his Prince, each developing scene of disgrace and abasement recalling the scenes of power. Cavendish in the first part tactfully reveals his awareness of Wolsey's vanity, Wolsey's unprincipled devotion to fulfilling the King's every whim in order to rise to power; and by thus showing himself capable of this detachment, he wins us to accept his sympathetic portrait of his master in disgrace.

Between the two great parts of the work, Cavendish projects a scene, beautifully bridging Wolsey's career, which dramatically symbolizes the violent change that has come over the Cardinal's fortunes and the simultaneous change, equally violent, that comes over Wolsey himself because his character has not been anchored in self-knowledge.

After the Cardinal-Chancellor has been suddenly bereft of his seals of office and must retire to his manor at Esher in Surrey, he crosses the Thames by barge to Putney and then he and his train take horse to finish their journey. At that instant Sir Harold Norris rides up with a royal message— Wolsey is not to think that the King is displeased with him. What follows, as shaped by Cavendish's pen, concentrates in a moment both the pathos of shattered greatness and the dislocation of personality in Wolsey's sudden fall:

"When he heard master Norris rehearse all the good and comfortable words of the King, he quickly lighted from his mule, all alone, as though he had been the youngest person among us. And incontinent kneeled down in the dirt upon both his knees, holding up his hands for joy. . . . And talking with master Norris on his knees in the mire, he would have pulled off his undercap of velvet, but he could not undo the knot under his chin. Wherefore with violence he rent the laces and pulled it from his head and so kneeled bareheaded."

Cavendish offers his credentials to the reader at the beginning of his work and movingly signs his warranty at the end. After he has given us the great scene of the Cardinal's deathbed, he reports that he went to the King, was well received, secured his wages, and rode away into retirement. By this deft touch—which at first glance seems a gratuitous intrusion of self—Cavendish quietly suggests that, in life, his service to Wolsey did not conflict with his duty to his sovereign, as, in the biography, his feeling for his master has not contravened his obligation to truth.

These two biographies have now received their just due in an exemplary edition (1962) issued by the Yale University Press. That they are combined within the covers of a single book is a happy stroke of publishing; for not only do they come into being about the same time and deal with the two most famous figures of Henry VIII's reign (1509–47) but, though Roper and Cavendish were not acquainted, the *Lives* complement each other so ironically that they seem almost to be the expression of a single biographical design.

More's remark to William Roper, "If my head could win him a castle in France, it should not fail to go" is balanced by Wolsey's cry uttered on his deathbed, "If I had served God as diligently as I have done the King, he would not have given me over in my gray hairs"—the same perception, but come too late. There are other moments in the two biographies as uncannily related. Roper records that More, after resigning the chancellorship, observed to the King's new favorite, Thomas Cromwell, "If you will follow my poor advice, you shall, in your counsel-giving unto His Grace, ever tell him what he ought to do but never what he is able to do. For if a lion knew his own strength, hard were it for any man to rule him." And Wolsey says, but has achieved the wisdom to say only as he dies, "He hath a princely heart; and rather than he will either miss or want any part of his will or appetite, he will put the loss of one half of his realm in danger." The biographies of Wolsey and More combine to create, we might almost say, a third biography, or at least character portrait, of the king they successively served as Chancellor.

It is a diverse field of biographical folk that we have surveyed in the first thousand years of the western world—Bishop Gregory of the Merovingian jungle; a monk, Einhard, buried in the darkness of the ninth century; an hysterical Margery Kempe; an old soldier; a flamboyant pope; a shrewd counsellor of kings; a scholar-lawyer; a gentleman-usher; a businessman who happened to be somebody's son-in-law—there are no discernible interconnections among them.

Poets read poets. Geoffrey Chaucer absorbed all the poetry of his age, the great French and Italian writers; Boccaccio looks to Petrarch and Dante; Wyatt and Surrey were startled into song by the power of Italian literature. But Margery Kempe did not know the work of Einhard; Cavendish had not read Commynes, nor did he and Roper know what the other was doing. Our field of folk are as innocent of such relationships as mushrooms mysteriously popping up on a lawn. Yet the works exhibit strong parallels, similarities achieved in darkness.

For one thing, these autobiographies and biographies offer a direct view of the awareness of their age and an indirect revelation of the direction in which men's minds are moving. We find in the fifteenth-sixteenth-century works the theme of counselling—Margery utters a strident sermon; Jean de Bueil tutors the aspirant soldier; the careerist, Aeneas Sylvius Piccolomini, becomes First Counsellor of Christendom; Commynes, adviser to Louis XI, has much to say about the proper education of a prince; More undertakes in his *History of Richard III* to counsel the kings of Europe, and he and Wolsey were both councillors to Henry VIII. What this theme of counsel reveals about the dawning Renaissance is its enlarged sense of human possibility, its increasing confidence in the plasticity of human experience, just as modern biography, for example, reveals our uncertainties about the science of psychoanalysis and our veneration for the science of facts en masse.

All the biographies represent a living conjunction of two

men, a life-relationship, which is transmuted into life-writing. The biographer himself is a part of the human experience which he is shaping into art. Such a conjunction will continue, until the twentieth century, to generate the chief ornaments of biographical composition.

Another striking resemblance lies in attitude toward the material, what we might call a professional awareness. In Chapter One I discussed some of the principal problems confronting the biographer, the solutions to which determine the nature and quality of any biography: the problem of viewpoint, the problem of truth, the problem of gaps, the problem of patterns.

The three autobiographies, for all the psychic distance separating them, are alike composed in the third person; only Pius II's choice was influenced by another work, Caesar's *Commentaries.* Though each autobiography adopts the third person for a different reason—Margery, as the signature of her humility; Bueil to disguise his originality; Aeneas to secure a freedom of self-display—the device is consciously employed as a means of imposing form upon autobiographical material.

All the biographers not only accept an obligation to be truthful but feel compelled to state this obligation and to present their credentials. Usually they create a personal envelope enwrapping their work, taking the reader into their confidence at both the beginning and the end. In thus disclosing their relationship with the subject, they establish point of view as well as give warranty for their reliability.

Einhard concludes his biography by transcribing the testament of Charlemagne, proof that he possesses intimate information. Commynes takes leave of the reader as he rides off, after the death of Charles VIII, to offer his services to Louis XII, a biographer who can be trusted because he had spent his life as the responsible councillor of kings. "I, William Roper," More's biographer begins, "though most unworthy, his son-in-law by marriage of his eldest daughter, knowing . . . no man living that of him and of his doings understood so much as myself, for that I was continually resident in his house by the space of sixteen years and more, thought it . . . my part to set forth such matters touching his life as I could at this present call to remembrance." Cavendish, in the same vein, declares, "Forsooth, this Cardinal was my lord and master, whom in his life I served, and so remained with him after his fall, continually during the term of all his trouble, until he died . . . and noted all his demeanor and usage [behavior] in all that time, as also in his wealthy [prosperous] triumph and glorious estate," and "therefore I commit the truth to Him that knows all truth . . ."

These biographers are likewise alert to the problem of gaps in the paper trail. Note how Einhard, far off in the ninth century, handles with disarming frankness a serious gap. "It would be folly, I think, to write a word concerning Charles' birth and infancy, or even his boyhood, for nothing has ever been written on the subject and there is no one alive now who can give information on it. Accordingly, I have determined to pass that by as unknown, and to proceed at once to treat of his character, his deeds, and such other facts of his life as are worth telling and setting forth . . ." Commynes frankly admits a similar disability in regard to Louis XI: "Of his youth I cannot speak, except from hearsay . . ."

All our biographers have shown themselves sensitive to the

problem of patterns. We have considered in some detail the array of forms and organizing-principles they devised in order to elicit the dominant rhythms and meanings of the lives they unfold.

Biography at the beginning of the modern world, like Athena sprung from the forehead of Zeus, makes its appearance full-grown. It will develop only by becoming increasingly ambitious, elaborate, and aware.

Henceforth, I shall continue only with the stream of modern English, and then English-American, biography. This span of life-writing exhibits notable growth and change, but—until the third decade of the twentieth century—nothing like the fulfillment which the achievements of the fifteenth century and the history of the other literary arts portend. It begins, in the Elizabethan Age, with an enigmatic blank, proceeds to a curiously flawed development in the seventeenth century, then to a brief triumph in the later eighteenth, followed by another disappointment in the nineteenth. Standard histories of biography have marked out the plots of ground; I shall seek only to indicate certain larger contours which have been less often noticed.

IV

Looking Back:
English Biography from the
Elizabethan Age to World War I

How can we account for the lack of biography in the Age of
Elizabeth, the last half of the sixteenth century? Here we are
confronted by one of the greatest literary efflorescences in the
history of mankind, and yet the period of the *Faerie Queene*
and *Hamlet* and Bacon's *Advancement of Learning* offers not
a single biography worthy of the name, much less a masterpiece.

Certainly the ground was prepared. Though Cavendish's
Life of Wolsey and Roper's *Life* of More remained in manuscript until the seventeenth century, it appears that those
manuscripts were known in literary circles. The fresh interest
in the drama of human life manifested in the fifteenth century
develops apace in the sixteenth. The Elizabethans were insa-
tiably curious about human beings, fascinated by the mystery

of personality. Shakespeare's "What a piece of work is a man" is echoed by Chapman's "Man is a torch, born in the wind." Jonson's comedies of humors expose the obsessions and irrationalities of human life. Burton's enormous disquisition upon melancholy signals the psychological inquisitiveness of the age. Translations of Plutarch and Suetonius, Shakespeare's triumphant use of Plutarch in his Roman plays and of biographical material from native chronicles in the history plays, all reveal public interest in great figures of the past; and the pamphlet literature of the day abounds in exuberant displays of personality. Yet, almost no biography.

We do find a life-relationship resulting in a biographical work. Fulke Greville, the author, was a talented man of letters, and the subject, his friend Sir Philip Sidney, is one of the most memorable characters of the time; but the result is lamentable—a feeble biographical effort deadened by stretches of political comment and moralizing.

Yet the age witnessed the first attempt at distinguishing biography as a thing-in-itself. Sir John Hayward noted the difference between historical writing and the writing of lives —but Sir John himself, the author of several studies of English kings, produced history instead of biography. The most brilliant mind of the period, Francis Bacon, likewise made this distinction. Unlike his contemporaries, Bacon was also quite aware of the lack of biography.

After declaring that a life, representing a person, is superior to history, representing a time, "in profit and use," Bacon observes, "For lives, I do find it strange that these times have so little esteemed the virtues of the times, as that the writing of lives should be no more frequent. For although there be not very many sovereign princes or absolute commanders, and that states are most collected into monarchies, yet are there many worthy personages that deserve better than dispersed report or barren elegies."

Bacon himself produced a *Life* of Henry VII, which is in many ways a distinguished work, but, alas, not a work of pure biography. It says nothing about Henry's earlier years, beginning with the moment that he defeats Richard III at Bosworth field and is crowned king; and although Bacon ends with a superb portrait of Henry as a monarch, most of the so-called life is actually a history of the reign. Bacon apparently recognized his failure to write a true biography of Henry VII, for in his dedication to Prince Charles, he pleads a paucity of materials: "I have not flattered him, but took him to life as well as I could, sitting so far off, and having no better light."

Bacon's excuse undoubtedly reveals one cause of this biographical lacuna: lack of information. Poets, playwrights, romancers were showered with materials—Italian and French and Spanish stories, translations from the classics, the medieval lore of Arthur and Charlemagne. Life-writing received no such encouragement. Government archives were neither readily accessible nor well-organized; sources like letters or journals were not yet generally preserved or if preserved were not regarded as spoils for a biographer. Literature had now fallen into the hands of professional men of letters; their noble patrons were above biography and their readers were unaware of it. Plutarch inspired the drama rather than biography; dramatic utterance was the idiom of the age.

Furthermore, it was dangerous to pursue the practice of biography. Writing the life of a private individual, like the playwright Shakespeare, for example, would have been safe enough; but Dr. Johnson's idea that the life of any man, projected with sufficient skill, would be interesting, had not yet occurred to anybody. Biographically, only great public figures counted, as the quotation from Bacon shows. And in the taut Elizabethan years of court intrigue, religious unrest, plots against the Queen, threats of foreign invasion, to write the life of a recently deceased public figure was an obviously risky enterprise. Because, in his work on Henry IV, he offered a frank discussion of Richard II's deposition, Sir John Hayward aroused the ire of Queen Elizabeth, and shortly thereafter found himself imprisoned in the Tower. If it was dangerous to deal with a figure dead for two hundred years, what would it be to write of a contemporary?

Ralegh touched shrewdly upon the point in the introduction to his *History of the World*. "Whosoever in writing a modern history shall follow truth too near the heels, it may haply strike out his teeth."

It may be also that the age was too exuberant for biography, as, in a different way, nineteenth-century America was too exuberant for biography. The Elizabethan period delighted in a luxuriance of language, in a proliferation of characters on the stage, in a pyrotechnic display of fancy in its poetry. Biography, on the other hand, must be chastened to truth, must accept galling limitations, must be content to shine in a sober light.

The age reached beyond truth for the grandiose—Spenser writing the *Faerie Queene* in order to "overgo Ariosto," Marlowe storming down from Cambridge to thrust his supermen upon the stage. Only the Italian complexities of Webster's

White Devil, only the brilliant violence of Chapman's *Bussy d'Ambois*, only the vast and mysterious psychological reaches of *Hamlet*, could satisfy the Elizabethans. Perhaps one life was too small.

The enigmatic blank of the Elizabethan Age was succeeded by an outburst of life-writing, as if that blank had represented an unnatural barrier, a suppression of biographical forces, which, under the weight of continuing scientific advances and enlarging self-consciousness, suddenly gave way.

But the biographical landscape of the seventeenth and early eighteenth century is bizarre and busy rather than richly productive, a time of experimentation and preparation. The life-writing impulse finds expression in a diversity of forms and a wide array of autobiographical activity—Theophrastan "characters," Plutarchan sketches, journals, memoirs, the diaries of Pepys and Evelyn, the self-examinations of Bunyan, the autobiographies of Lord Herbert of Cherbury and Colley Cibber, and, by the earlier eighteenth century, a spate of sensational *exposés*, lives of criminals, pseudo-confessions, slanderous tracts.

Of biography springing from a relationship in life the age offers three curiosities and a masterpiece. Lady Fanshawe produced a life of her ambassador-husband; Mrs. Hutchinson, one of her warrior-husband; and the uninhibited Duchess of Newcastle, one of her Duke, an amiable mediocrity. The Duchess still makes good reading: she rushed into biography as a bride hurls herself into her husband's arms.

The masterpiece is Roger North's biographies of his three brothers—Francis, the Lord Chief Justice, "my best brother";

the merchant-adventurer, Sir Dudley; and the neurotic scholar, John.

Roger North was a man of two dominant passions: his passion for his family and his passion for the practice of biography; and he fused them into a single purpose. In addition to the lives of his three brothers, he wrote an autobiography, and as a preface to the life of Francis, the Lord Chief Justice, he produced the first extensive critical essay on biography—which has only recently been published, in excerpts, by James Clifford—wherein he anticipates many of the chief ideas of Johnson and Boswell.

North is at his best in recreating, by means of vividly realized moments, the warmth of personality. He is at his liveliest in writing of his brother Dudley, who went to Turkey to make his fortune. "Our merchant, after he found his heart's ease at Constantinople . . . began to grow fat, which increased upon him till, being somewhat tall, and well whiskered, he made a jolly appearance, such as the Turks approve most of all in a man." On Dudley's return to England, "When first he came over, I kept a sailing-yacht upon the Thames; and the first time we took him aboard, he clapped himself down upon the seat by the helm, and, taking the whipstaff in his hand, *by God*, said he, *I'll be admiral;* and there he sat, and steered, with all the delight imaginable."

Roger North's lives of his three brothers are the most richly developed biographies that had so far been written in England.

The seventeenth century likewise produced the first approach to a professional biographer in Izaak Walton, whose lives of Donne and Wotton and Herbert and Hooker and

Sanderson are widely known and have been highly praised. Walton, unfortunately, tends to endow his subjects, even passionate John Donne, with something of the genteel and whimsical piety that so characterized himself. He smooths out too many wrinkles and planes off too many rough edges of his people. Nevertheless he builds his biographical portraits with great skill.

The age produced another quasi-professional biographer, but one who spent all his energies gathering material, and was never quite able to work the material up into a biography. John Aubrey, in his *Brief Lives*, displays what can only be called an ineluctable flair for uncovering personality. He is a Suetonius *manqué*. He had the nervous system of a biographer; all he lacked was application. What he wrote of himself in 1666 serves as a kind of motto of his character—"All my businesses and affairs ran kim kam." It would almost serve as a motto for this century, in which what we might call the biographical opportunity does not seem to have been fully realized. Somehow the cross-play of the intellectual concerns of the age acted as a prism, shattering the light of life-writing into sparkles, rather than as a lens to focus it.

The latter part of the eighteeth century achieves what the previous hundred and fifty years had been, it would seem, groping toward. We find a profuse display of all kinds of biographical writing: autobiography achieves literary form in the self-portraits of Edward Gibbon and Benjamin Franklin; there emerges the first eminent professional English biographer, Dr. Samuel Johnson; finally, the most famous of all biographical conjunctions produces the world's greatest biography, Boswell's *Life of Johnson*.

Johnson's services to biography and the triumph of Boswell's *Life* have been too thoroughly and justly elucidated to require comment here. Each year sees the appearance of more books and articles about Johnson and Boswell than about all the rest of our biographical heritage.

Boswell's incomparable interweaving of diurnalness with the grand patterns of a complex personality and the grand rhythms of a highly sentient and articulate existence marvelously recreates the sense of a life being lived. The Age of Enlightenment in England receives perhaps its fullest psychological expression in this work, as that Age represents in civilized awareness the cumulative development of four hundred years.

But Boswell's *Johnson* is more than a consolidation of gains. For all that it seems to epitomize so many social-intellectual conventions of the eighteenth century—for example, the devotion to urban life, confidence in common sense, approval of the "clubbable" man—this extravagant pursuit of a biographical object, this laying bare of a man's pungent eccentricities, grotesqueries, madnesses, this flamboyant proclamation of the importance of an individual, speaks a prophetic language. It is surely part of that great revolution in consciousness, ideas, attitudes, signaled by the *Memoirs* of Voltaire, the *Confessions* of Rousseau, the fall of the Bastille, the writings of Hume and Kant and Tom Paine. This revolution seemed to offer a happy prospect to biography; for that art, dealing directly with personality exhibited as behavior and with consciousness expressed in experience, should be quick to respond to new, heady views about the self and the world.

And yet the prospect soon clouded over.

In the new nation which had emerged from the Thirteen Colonies it was as though the romantic quest for identity, the exploration of personality trembling into wonder, had not crossed the ocean, as if Boswell had never written his *Life of Johnson*. Distinguished American writers from Washington Irving and Nathaniel Hawthorne to Henry James published biographies, but they are of no importance. Until the First World War the United States is, biographically speaking, virtually a blank.

There appeared one competent professional biographer, James Parton, whose many works were seriously researched and composed with conscious artistry. Parton's first biography, a *Life* of Horace Greeley (1855)—which he undertook as the result of a chance conversation with a publisher in a restaurant—sold 30,000 copies within a few months of publication. Parton then devoted his writing career to biography, and in such *Lives* as his *Burr* and *Jefferson* and *Jackson* created vigorous, fluent biographical narratives. Mid-nineteenth-century America, however, offered small rewards to a man earning a living by his pen. "The best way is to make a fortune first and write afterwards," Parton once observed. He is a little like Edgar Allan Poe, a man driven to hackwork and hasty writing in order to keep the pot boiling. Even his best works are now in discard, outmoded by modern scholarship and forgotten by the reading public.

Of biography growing out of a life relationship, there is nothing of value. The rest of the story is more or less demand-biography—lives of eminent leaders, statesmen and warriors and preachers and pioneers. Perhaps the young country needed the reassurance provided by heroes and patriotic sentiment, while its energies were absorbed into the making of the nation. But the United States produced first-rate novelists and short-story writers, a world poet in Whitman—why not great biography?

If such works had appeared, how easy it would be to explain them. The magnificent display of human vitality produced by the conquest of a continent, the emphasis on freedom and individual responsibility on the frontier, the stimulus of an egalitarian but acquisitive society, the blaze of great talents thrown up by the challenges of the new world—Jefferson, Emerson, Thoreau, Lincoln—all these forces, fertilized by the consummation of the biographical art in Boswell's *Life of Johnson* made it inevitable that nineteenth-century America should create great biography. But it did not happen.

Victorian England offers, in a way, an even greater disappointment. Before we explore it, let me record two ironies-at-large in the biographical panorama stretching a century and a half from post-Boswell to present-day England.

The era of English life-writing between the French Revolution and World War One and the era of English life-writing from World War One to the present both got under way with a spectacular explosion, even as did the other literary arts: Romanticism, on the one hand; an upheaval of multi-isms on the other.

At the opening of the nineteenth century, the revolution in human attitudes and values—sounding in the *Jupiter* symphony, the guns of Marengo, clanking looms in Lancashire, a purling of *Lyrical Ballads*, the strident *Confessions* of J. J.

Rousseau, Delphic utterances of German philosophy—this psychological revolution, richly seeded the germination-beds of English life-writing; and there in the sky stood the warming sun of Boswell's *Life of Johnson* to start the seeds into life.

All forms of life-writing burgeoned—retrospective and introspective essays, reveries, Coleridge on Coleridge and Henry Crabb Robinson on everybody, diaries, journals, autobiographies, biographies. The very word *autobiography* now, apparently, comes into being (1797 in the *Monthly Review*). Many of the literary figures write biographies or have biographies written about them. Haydon, painting for immortality, keeps a journal to make sure his intention is not misunderstood. The great produce autobiographies and their friends cobble at memoirs.

Yet, long before Alfred Tennyson, after a whirlwind courtship of seventeen years, marries Emily Sellwood and publishes *In Memoriam* in 1850, the promise of biography, for all of Boswell's *Johnson* and the heady psychological drafts of Romanticism, has faded into humdrum performance, pseudobiography. What one could confidently have prophesied in the year of Waterloo—a golden fulfillment of eighteenth-century biographical development—did not materialize.

On the other hand, the second revolution in values and attitudes, coming after World War One, promised nothing like so much for biography as the first; and the new sun in the sky, Lytton Strachey, was certainly a minor luminary compared to James Boswell. Indeed, in the first dozen years or so following the war it appeared as if the journalists and the Stracheyites and the Third-Monarchy Men of psychoanalysis would bury biography altogether. Yet from this seemingly unhappy revolution, biographically speaking, there has developed the art of life-writing of our day, which, I venture to suggest, in general standard of achievement, if not in masterpieces, must be given pre-eminent place in English and American biographical history.

In the case of what happened to biography in the Victorian Age, the outlines, at least, of the story are quite clear.

Under the powerful stimulus of Boswell's *Johnson*, biography attracted great talents at the opening of the nineteenth century. That stimulus stemmed partly from the example of what we might loosely call the Boswell formula—the artful interweaving of materials drawn directly from the subject's letters, journals, conversations—but probably even more from the sheer inspiration of Boswell's accomplishment, the testimony that in recreating the life of a man, a biographer might achieve a work of high literary art and lasting impact.

The chief biographies that came into being in these years are paraded, quickly, through all the literary histories: Scott's *Life of Dryden*, Southey's *Lives* of Nelson and Wesley, Moore's *Byron*, Lockhart's elaborate *Life of Scott*. Then, as we pass 1840, the procession thins out: Carlyle's *Sterling*, a slight work; Mrs. Gaskell's *Charlotte Brontë*; Trevelyan's *Macaulay*; Froude's *Carlyle*; Forster's *Dickens*—a mere handful of titles over a span of sixty years. And we end with Morley's monumental, that is, stone-cold, *Life of Gladstone*.

By the 1840's the cultural-social forces of the age had throttled the development of biography. These forces, which we encompass under the too-large term, *Victorianism*, have been studied in detail; their effect upon life-writing is clear to behold; and I shall quickly move to certain ancillary considerations. As Sir Harold Nicolson pointed out a generation ago, "Then came earnestness, and with earnestness hagiography descended on us with its sullen cloud, and the Victorian biographer scribbled laboriously by the light of shaded lamps." Along with moral earnestness, Sir Harold singles out the "deep belief in a personal deity" as "responsible for the catastrophic failure of Victorian biography." This diagnosis needs some adjustment. In other ages "deep belief" has not impeded life-writing; and it would be truer to describe the period as one of anxious doubt. The chief forces working against biography were consciously applied: a social image of respectability generated by the ambitious but prudent middle class, and the psychological image of man as a decorous animal which was created to bolster the social image. A gap opened then between what man knew of man—the hard-won advances of three centuries—and what man permitted himself to know.

All the arts were affected but none so seriously as biography, for biography was affected in its vitals: biography deals directly with the actualities of human life. William Roper, in the sixteenth century, did not tell all he knew about Thomas More, but he told everything that he thought was important to tell. In the Victorian Age, what was known to be important in a life had become enormously enlarged; but what was permissible to acknowledge had shrunk to the innocuous, padded with didactic observations. Whereas life-writing demands candor, candor is the essential condition of its being, the age insisted on a simulacrum of life, and the more famous the man, the more varnished the exemplum: the husband, devoted; the father, loving; the citizen, public-spirited; and the gentleman, Christian.

Biography was silenced; pseudobiography took its place. The steam press had arrived to print it; the spread of education produced an ever-growing public to read it; and the periodicals loyally offered domesticated reviewers to approve it. Just as the age enjoyed vast meals, long sermons and heavy whiskies, it consumed with relish the marmoreal two-volume pseudobiography, commissioned, sometimes written, by the widow—witness what Lady Burton, her pen guided by the *zeitgeist,* did to her wild and wonderful husband. Whiskers hid the Victorian face no more securely than pseudobiography hid the Victorian heart. And just as biographical energies were perverted to eulogy, so critical energies—what few such energies were applied to biography—expended themselves upon just one tiresome question—what limited truth is to be permitted in life-writing?

Poets, novelists, could exercise choice, school the imagination, suggest what they could not say, and, checked by an adamantine frontal position, turn the flank. They might be harassed, limited, even maimed, but they could still write poetry, novels. Biography had no such choice: it was silence or pseudo-. After all, Thackeray could tell the whole truth about Becky Sharp because only so much of Becky existed as Thackeray invented. But Stanley in his absurd *Life* of Thomas Arnold and Mrs. Gaskell in her finely wrought *Life* of Charlotte Brontë told very much less than the truth because they, as biographers, and the lives they dealt with, had been taken into the protective custody of the age.

There was a Gothic Revival in more than the architectural

sense. Biography became a neo-hagiography, a return to the biographical condition of the Middle Ages, to the dominance of demand-biography (which, of course, exists in all ages), that is, to life-writing determined by the pressures of society rather than by the pressures of talent, the exigencies of the medium, and the self-consciousness of the times.

Mention of the Middle Ages brings us to an aspect of the nineteenth-century plight of biography which has not been much noticed. That plight can be usefully viewed, I believe, as developing from the conflict of two forces: the psychological awareness achieved by the age and the "received attitude" toward human life of the age. At all times, life-writing, which lives by the former, has been ineluctably conditioned by the latter. In a measure, the quality of life-writing in any era is determined by this relationship of these two forces.

For example, by the fifth century A.D., the general psychological awareness achieved by pagan Graeco-Roman culture was strikingly fertilized by the revolutionary conception of personality developed by Christianity. As we have seen, this happy mating flashes into life-writing in the *Confessions* of Augustine. But the *Confessions* do not, as might have been supposed, open up a fruitful era of biography. On the contrary, genuine biography is in that age extinguished. What happened was that triumphant Christianity established an "official" view of man in which biography could serve only as an instrument for the propagation of the faith. The advance in awareness of personality was nullified by the very cultural force which made it possible; thus the *Confessions* are followed only by celebrations of martyrdoms and inspiring stories of holy-men; and biography is lost in the thousand-year night of saints' lives.

In the fifteenth and early sixteenth centuries, on the contrary, a native psychological awareness, slowly opening outward over many centuries and now quickened by humanism, is able to express itself biographically because the medieval "official" view of man is weakening, is being infiltrated by a view of man that encourages life-writing. As a result, there comes into being that array of biographical writings we have already examined, from Margery Kempe's *Autobiography* to Cavendish's *Life* of Wolsey.

While the failure of Victorian biography is a unique phenomenon, it springs from a collision of forces which, throughout history, have shaped the destinies of life-writing. We shall see, similarly, that the biographical recovery of the twentieth century arises from a double alteration: a dramatically enlarged awareness (which, however, was developing in the nineteenth) and a change in the established attitude toward man.

To return, for a moment, to those well-known titles I have mentioned, from Lockhart's *Scott* to Froude's *Carlyle* —it is time, I think, that their actual status today should be admitted. They are embalmed in our literary histories, a petrified forest. They are not a living part of us; and when we set them beside their predecessors, we quickly perceive that they are not read as Roper's *Life* of More is read, or even as Roger North's *Lives* of his three brothers are read. They have been superseded by twentieth-century works which may lack the immediacy of their scenes drawn from memory and even, in some cases, their artistry, but which come nearer to the actuality of the subject.

Even these eminent *Lives* partly succumbed to the age.

They tell something like the truth, with discretion; the truth but not the whole truth; occasionally not even that. Lockhart, for example, tries to persuade us that he is always giving us the real Walter Scott, whereas, by deliberate distortions and omissions, he sometimes gives us instead that established figure, the genial Wizard of the North. Yet, be it noted, these biographers, from Lockhart to Froude, were virulently attacked, accused of besmirching their heroes, of ghoulishly plundering the dead, etc. Sulphurous Thomas Carlyle remarked, "How delicate, how decent, is English biography, bless its mealy mouth!"

Finally, it must also be noted that most of these works spring, like Boswell's *Johnson*, from a living relationship between the biographer and his subject, the relationship which produced almost all the great biographies written prior to the Victorian era.

What was stifled, then, in the featherbed of Victorian propriety was not a new form, a fresh approach, an original conception of biography, but a rising standard of biographical excellence, inspired by Boswell's *Johnson* and continuing the main line of the English biographical tradition.

The life-writing impulse, suppressed or perverted, the biographical awareness of the age, hobbled, found other means and guises of expression. It seems hardly fanciful to suggest that the splendid procession of nineteenth-century novels which assume the form of a life, represent, in part at least, the idiom of biography finding vent in fiction—*David Copperfield*, *Pendennis*, *Jane Eyre*, *The Way of All Flesh*, and the like.

There is no question that Victorian biographical energies were turned to all manner of industrious busy-work, of varying worth, to the classifying of information, to the large-scale accumulation of materials: *Lives of the Lord Chancellors; Lives of the Lord Chief Justices; The English Men of Letters* series; the *Dictionary of National Biography;* Camden Society, Early English Text Society, and other "Society" publications; reports of the Royal Manuscripts Commission; calendaring of government documents; the appearance of the *Greville Memoirs, The Croker Papers, The Creevy Papers,* etc. Enormous biographical compilations—they are not biographies—come into being. David Masson produced his *Life of Milton Narrated in Connection with the Political, Ecclesiastical, and Literary History of his Time,* in six massive volumes; while James Spedding outdid him with seven volumes of Bacon's Works, Papers, Speeches, and seven more volumes of *Life and Letters*—Carlyle called the first seven volumes the "hugest and faithfulest bit of literary navvy-work" of the age. Nothing like such extensive biographical excavation had been known before—awareness driven underground to mine for ore.

It is autobiography, however, that furnishes the experimental, adventurous manifestations of nineteenth-century lifewriting. In the biographical burgeoning of the earlier years Wordsworth, standing on the psychological advances and the autobiographical promptings of the late eighteenth century, created in *The Prelude* an exploration of his spiritual development which opened new vistas of autobiography. Byron's *Childe Harold,* III and IV, exuberantly record the interaction of a personality and its world. The autobiographical chapters of Carlyle's *Sartor Resartus* likewise create windows on the panorama of self. Poetry as a vehicle for formal autobiography, or segment thereof, is not new, but neither is it common. One of the early Fathers, Gregory of Nazianzus, turned to verse to express the frustrations of dealing with a turbulent flock. Thomas Occleve in the *Male Règle* produced one of the few fresh poetic utterances of the fifteenth century. But the *Prelude* is another world. Its simultaneous investigation and evocation of self take us a giant stride in the history of autobiography.

Furthermore, the *Prelude,* the *Sartor Resartus* chapters, and, for that matter, that lesser autobiographical segment, Tennyson's *In Memoriam,* are all developed in terms of a dramatic psychological pattern (European Romanticism incarnate), what has been called "withdrawal and return": the young organism, fired by illusion and hope, collides with the world, and, desperately wounded in its beliefs and aspirations, recoils into the cave of despair; but, after black days, healing sets in, and a mature individual eventually emerges, at least in some measure restored, to do battle with existence.

Throughout our period, until World War One, autobiography continues to outstrip biography in its bold grapplings with aspects of self and the means of revealing it. Since autobiography is a freer form than biography—not so decisively anchored to an outward reality, enjoying the license of retrospect and the privacy of self-examination, a fantasia on the theme of life—it continued to escape the smother of the Victorian Age by experiments in limited intentions and thematic discipline.

Thematic autobiography, of course, goes back a long way.

The *Confessions* of Augustine are narrowly thematic, a life compressed to the birth of a Christian soul, as in a relaxed, jolly way the *Autobiography* of Ben Franklin is thematic, the making of a success. But the autobiographies I shall now mention progressively develop a thematic attack on the problems of the genre with an acute self-consciousness and a sophistication of form never before achieved.

Newman's beautifully articulated *Apologia* tenaciously disentangles one grand strand of experience, its chastity of selection providing an almost poetic commentary upon the meaning. The *Autobiography* of J. S. Mill, severely analytical, ruthless in its excision of the movements of the outer life, unfolds the "record of an education which was unusual and remarkable," emphasizing the "successive phases" of intellectual development. This autobiography finds a partner in the United States in the bleak quest of *The Education of Henry Adams*.

Then, in 1907, appeared a brilliantly original work, which, both in its thematic conception and in its literary realization, carries autobiography still further, *Father and Son* by Edmund Gosse. This autobiographical-biographical study of two generations in conflict, the Victorian father hardened in dogma and the rebellious son touched by the new science, is developed with the resources of the novel and from a viewpoint both compassionate and detached.

The yell of outrage which greeted *Father and Son* showed that the Victorian Age was still alive and kicking. The *Times Literary Supplement* review began, "The author of this book has no doubt settled it with his conscience how far in the interests of popular edification and amusement it is legitimate to expose the weaknesses and inconsistencies of a good man who is also one's father." While Sir Sidney Lee was declaring, as late as 1911, that life-writing should offer matter "which stirs and firmly holds the attention of the earnest-minded," Edmund Gosse, in his article in the *Britannica*, defined biography as "the faithful portrait of a soul in its adventures through life."

Finally, autobiography in this era reaches the apogee of its search for freedom-and-discipline through theme and in its increasingly rich means of expression in George Moore's complex, whimsical, and quasi-novelized assertion of self, *Hail and Farewell*, three volumes. This work is limited in space and time to Moore's ten-year adventure with the Irish Renascence and is keyed to one dominant idea, the necessity of freeing Ireland from the Church so that Irish art may flourish. Reverie, flashback, scene, psychological montage, daring economy of transition—these devices which we associate with the novel of the time—are deployed in *Hail and Farewell* in the service of autobiography. The ostentatious manipulation, the narrowness and even aridity of the theme, and the somewhat uncertain appeal of the substance itself have perhaps unduly weighed against this ingenious work—what one would be tempted to call a pioneering venture, except that there are no wagon-trains to follow.

Though published in 1914, only three years before *Eminent Victorians*, Moore's experimental autobiography will have no such effect as Strachey's biographical studies. As we shall see, it is a culmination, and in many ways an end, of autobiographical development rather than a harbinger.

V

Contemporary Biography

IF MODERN BIOGRAPHY began with a book, Boswell's *Johnson*, contemporary biography in England and America began with a bang—the guns of the First World War blowing to pieces so many of the men and the states and the attitudes and the values of the Victorian world. The arts, already in ferment before the outbreak of that war, led the cry against Victorianism, proclaimed the arrival of liberation, experimentation, an exhilarating new day by the light of which man and his institutions would be reinterpreted, his enlarged powers given new expression. All sorts of *isms* burst into existence, expanded, and exploded—Dadaism and neo-expressionism and Freudianism . . .

Biography could not resist these volcanic forces. In the general upheaval of the arts, biography upheaved itself also. What Schoenberg and his twelve-tone system were doing for music, and Eugene O'Neill was doing for drama, Lytton Strachey did for biography in the publication of *Eminent Victorians* in 1917 and then, a few years later, his *Life of Queen Victoria*.

Strachey's brilliant, sophisticated attack upon Victorianism hoisted a shining banner in the wind of change. He demonstrated that biography, too, could be exciting, could express the personality of the writer, could join in the joyous iconoclasm, and could sell. A host of imitators sprang up. Debunking biographers laid low the heroic figures of the past, exuberantly proving that marble statues had feet of clay. Freudian biographers excitedly dug into the kitchen-midden of suppressions and complexes like schoolboys playing at archeology. Fictionizers sought to secure Strachey's effects, but lacking his genius, freely invented materials in order to demonstrate their talents and please the public.

It was a gay party while it lasted, but the favors were cheap and quickly shredded and the refreshments lacked sustenance. Before the end of the thirties, the "new" biography had lost its savor; critics like Bernard DeVoto and Allan Nevins exposed the shabbiness of amateurish psychoanalytical writing and the public turned its face away.

Meanwhile, the genuine accomplishment of Lytton Strachey had become recognized. His ironic detachment from his material, his lacquered style, his delicacy of selection and his dramatic touch, all left a permanent mark upon biography. Furthermore, biography had become a subject for serious literary examination. Harold Nicolson produced his perceptive little volume, *The Development of English Biography*; André Maurois joined the discussion with his *Aspects of Biography*; and dedicated people of letters like Virginia Woolf likewise responded to this critical interest in life-writing. In the United States, Gamaliel Bradford's impressionistic biographical sketches, which he called psychographs, stimulated interest in the possibilities of the medium, and Wilbur Cross in his *Lives* of Laurence Sterne and Henry Fielding had showed the academic world that scholarly biography need not lack grace and style.

The movement of criticism was of brief duration and has been followed only by sporadic sallies; but by the coming of the Second World War, the art of biography had steadied, had found its twentieth-century voice, and has since assumed a firmly recognized, if hardly dominant, place on the literary scene. Between 1916 and 1930, about 4800 biographies were published in the United States, averaging something like 300 a year. In 1929, at the height of the biographical boom, 667 new biographical works appeared, in a country of about 120 million people. In 1962, for a population of 180 million people, exactly the same number of new biographies was published, out of a total of 16,448 titles. In Great Britain in 1962, 577 biographies appeared among the 18,975 new books which came from the presses. Biography is not often to be found in the best-seller lists, nor is it a notable winner of literary prizes; it has not produced an array of masterpieces. Yet it can be argued that life-writing at present, both in England and America, is practiced with a greater skill and devotion than at any time in its history.

The influence of Lytton Strachey, inspirational and technical, was quickly diffused into the biographical atmosphere. In the long run his work has served to reflect rather than to alter the intellectual climate which plays upon biography. The shape and quality of modern life-writing owes most to the large forces which have determined the destiny of all the arts.

Of modern self-consciousness I need not speak. We are the

inheritors of scientific advances begun in the early seventeenth century and enormously accelerated in the early twentieth. To call this, even in irony, the Age of Freud, indicates
our consciousness of, and doubts about, self and personality.
All sorts of keys to human behavior have been handed to the
biographer—which, it is true, he has sometimes used to open
the wrong door, or has thrown away, or has played with like a
small boy, uttering squeals of delight. As for an "official,"
socially imposed view of man—in all degrees of voice, profound to superficial, from all the licensed explainers of existence, philosophers and sociologists and preachers and econo-
mists and literary critics, society has been offered so many
candidates for an official view of man, ranging from despair to
euphoria, that, for biography, the field is wide open. There is
no official view, as in the nineteenth century, to conflict with
our level of self-consciousness. Yet, within this framework of
awareness unrestrained, if not unharassed, two powerful
forces have pressed upon life-writing: the force of science and
the force of literature, one from without, as it were, and one
from within.

Let us turn, for the moment, to two illustrative prophecies,
written about 1930, regarding the course that biography was
to pursue.

Hesketh Pearson, one of the most prolific of English professional biographers, declared exuberantly, "Already we
have a school of biographers who are displacing the dramatists
and novelists of pre-war days. . . . It is the day of the biographer; he is the dramatist, the essayist, the romanticist of the
future . . ." Perhaps it is as well for literature that this bac-
chic augury has proved wide of the mark.

Towards the close of his *Development of English Biography*, Sir Harold Nicolson predicted that "the scientific interest in biography is hostile to and will in the end prove destructive of the literary interest. . . . The more biography becomes a branch of science, the less will it become a branch of literature. The literary element will, of course, persist, but it will be driven into other directions . . ."

With clairvoyance, he singled out the two forces, scientific and literary, which in the succeeding generation have indeed exerted a decisive influence upon biography. The influence, however, has not been so drastically or unrelievedly unfortunate as Sir Harold predicted. Both the force of science and the force of literature have turned out to be Janus-headed, malign *and* beneficial—and biography has in many ways profited from an invigorating, though dangerous, whip-saw of countercurrents.

In Great Britain, this split between science and literature in biography is much less severe than in the United States, just as, in the novel, the most spectacular adventures of modern fiction can be more clearly viewed here than in England. The steadier balance of English intellectual society, the slower metabolic rate of the English temperament, English reluctance to climb on the band-wagon of science, the continuing force exerted by the Oxbridge tradition of civilized letters, and the dedicated amateurism of the British—they play games, make indexes, and regard facts more casually than Americans—have all contributed, I believe, to reduce the extremes of the American biographical condition. The scholar, Miss C. V. Wedgwood, for example, writes so beautifully that we are not distracted by her learning, while the writer,

Lord David Cecil, let us say, researches so meticulously that we are not played false by his style. Great Britain and the United States both have their share of distinguished works, competent biographical writing, and ephemeral or indigestible biographies; but the emphatic polarity of American biography reveals more vividly the impact of modern social-cultural forces.

The force of science has exerted a wide range of pressures on life-writing. It has, in general, stimulated the researcher behind the biographer to higher standards of precision and thoroughness than have hitherto been observed. In published source-materials—letters, journals, historical documents—no editions of the nineteenth or early twentieth century can be trusted; whereas today accuracy can be taken for granted in the work of all responsible scholars. Serious biographers have been spurred by the prevailing reverence for "the scientific approach" to seek out their evidences with dogged persistence, to eschew second-hand materials and concentrate upon the original document, the actual letter, to view with skepticism all doubtful information however attractive, and to interpret their findings with a rigorous regard for the elusiveness of truth.

Indirectly, science has provided aid and comfort for biography through that proliferating institution, the University, where the most intense scientific activity is concentrated and where its prestigious practitioners give the law. In the United States the writing of biography has been increasingly domesticated on the campus, as librarians, English departments, historians, have succeeded in diverting to themselves ever larger tributaries of the golden flow nourishing research. The professor-biographer—and most of the best American biographies are now probably written by professors—enjoys a financial support and technical aids that would have been a marvel to James Parton. Funds are available—after test tubes and reactors have been provided for—to buy microprinters, microfilm, xerographs, photostats, stenographic and research assistance, even leisure for study and writing.

Leaves-of-absence, with pay, are supplemented by grants from national bodies such as the American Council of Learned Societies; by fellowships from foundations, particularly the Guggenheim Foundation, which has done so much for so many scholars of all varieties, including biographers; and by aids and services of many sorts provided by the great libraries, like the Folger in Washington under the imaginative direction of that scholar-artist, Louis B. Wright. University librarians buy biographical materials right and left, hire people to catalogue them, install electronic retrieval systems to make them instantly accessible; university presses stand ready to print those biographies whose appeal is too limited for the commercial publishers; and university communities harbor the bookstores and the public on which the biographer mainly depends for his slender royalties.

Under the aegis of science, the American biographer, then, has received support and encouragement which are the envy of his fellows in the rest of the world.

On the other hand, the force of science has fastened biography in a bear-hug—dangerous today, perhaps frightening for tomorrow. Science, wittingly or no, has pressed us—and "us" includes biographers—to worship information as a thing-in-itself, to acknowledge the supremacy of facts and therefore to regard the accumulation of facts, no matter what kind, as the highest good; to confuse research—the ferreting out of facts —with scholarship, the understanding of them; to put our trust in methods, statistics, machinery. Attitudes proper to the physical sciences, and perhaps necessary to the newer ambitious sciences, have been diffused as standards of value for all manner of research. The vast collecting of data by, let us say, anthropology and by biology, the statistical measurements of sociology, garnering mass responses to experience, mass patterns of behavior, have stimulated a magpie competition in the weight, bulk, complexity of fact-compilation.

We pack into cavernous, air-filtered archives every scrap of information about ourselves, and we ransack the past for every scrap of information about our forebears. Indefatigable Frankensteins, in order to tame this monster before it crushes us, we organize scholarly "factories" and "laboratories" and "teams" in order to catalogue the precious detritus of the centuries and arrange it for publication. At Yale, proud plumes of smoke rise from the famous chimneys of the Boswell factory and the Johnson factory and the Walpole factory; many another university has, or is building, its historical and literary factories.

In themselves, the best of these enterprises offer humane services which mock mockery. The letters of Horace Walpole, the papers of Thomas Jefferson, given to the world in handsome volumes, admirably edited, offer an enrichment to life in general as well as immense aid to the labors of future scholars. Yet, for the art of biography, precariously perched between the demand of fact and the hope of illumination, this ambience of mass attack upon mass materials, of fact triumphant, has already posed, as we shall see, the threat of paralysis.

However, one branch of science, casting a spell on all the arts, has offered opportunties to the twentieth-century biographer which have wonderfully enlarged and enlightened the whole domain of life-writing. How could it be otherwise?—the science of human behavior speaks directly to him who seeks to puzzle out the unfolding of a life. Psychology and psychoanalysis have thrust fingers of light into the cave of the human mind, have deepened our sense of the complexities, the arcane tides, of personality, have enabled us to penetrate some of the dark corners of motive and desire, to detect patterns of action, and sense the symbolic value of word and gesture.

The biographer need not, fortunately, be a psychoanalyst, or even a student of psychoanalysis, to draw profit from the science. Merely as twentieth-century educated man he shares an insight into human nature veiled from his predecessors. Indeed, if he applies himself too intently to psychology, he runs the danger, unless he subdues his knowledge to his literary purpose, of producing a clinical exposition of a subject instead of the Life of a man. As Mark Schorer has observed, "A biographer, like any other civilized man, should know about the developments of modern psychology, but I do not think he should write as if he were a psychoanalyst."

Psychoanalysis is, after all, *analysis;* it explains, provides names for, classifies, deals in clinical record. But a biography is not *about* a man's life; it is the simulation of that life in words. When the biographer deploys his psychological knowledge or aspirations thereto, upon the page, he is telling

instead of showing, he is transforming his subject into a specimen, he is blotting out the sense of a life being lived—the
supreme object of biography—in order to deliver a lecture.
The biographer's relations with psychology had better be pla-
tonic; she is an invaluable friend but as mistress, a *femme
fatale*.

Psychology has also produced secondary radiation effects,
probably slight, on the biographical climate. The bread-
earning emphasis, in applied psychology, on psychic "types,"
frameworks and catch-alls of character, automatic diagnosis
by psychological "profiles," has reinforced the general atmosphere of dehumanization exuded by statistical sciences like
sociology; and that atmosphere, at the least, has made it
harder for the biographer, one man at grips with one man, to
catch his breath.

The force of literature, the "literary element," as Nicolson
puts it, has not exerted nearly so dramatic an influence as the
force of science; but that influence has, in all probability, been
more steadily beneficial than baneful.

The biographer has been stimulated by the novelist—who
in the United States is also likely to be a campus inhabitant—
to develop literary as well as scholarly ambitions and to pay
increasing attention to the formal problems of unfolding a
life. Not infrequently these days the biographer is, like Mark
Schorer and Leon Edel, a critic or writer of fiction, or, like
Miss C. V. Wedgwood in Great Britain, an historian who is
also a distinguished woman of letters. Professor-biographers
have been moved to realize not only that Lives must be as
artfully written as they are ardently researched but that biography demands not the exposition but the projection, the dram-

atization, of a life.

Yet literature, too, has played Mr. Hyde as well as Dr. Jekyll, or rather, has shown a temptress' as well as a help-meet's face. The modern novel has had an excitingly experimental career. It has generated all manner of new devices to tell old stories, has dared any manipulation of time, any violence of viewpoint, any innovations in narrative that offered possibilities of enriching, or enlivening, the domain of fiction. The serious biographer, on the other hand, is confined within the adamantine limits of the biographic oath to tell the truth. With enlarged means, it is true, and with an enlarged understanding of his medium, he is doing much the same thing that Einhard and Roger North were doing; whereas the present-day spinner of stories is working a much different vein, exploring quite another world, from those of the creator of Icelandic Sagas or even from those of Daniel Defoe.

The writer who is biographically inclined, eyeing the multi-coursed feast of the novelist, has reached for goodies beyond a biographer's power to digest, has sometimes indeed claimed the right to sit at the table and quaff the Falernian of invention. As the pressure of science threatens to smother the biographer in fact, the enticements of literature threaten to over-stimulate him with artifices.

This climate of attitudes and impulsions has done much to shape the three chief characteristics of modern American and British life-writing: (1) the decline of autobiography and the concomitant decline of biography springing from a life-relationship; (2) the extraordinarily wide range of biographical literature; and (3) the development of a mode of biographical composition, not hitherto entirely unknown perhaps, but new as a self-conscious practice.

Autobiographical *activity* has certainly not declined. "Ghosted" pot-boilers and artless effusions explore all latitudes from the doldrums of *Fifty Years in the Indian Civil Service* and the windy reaches of *Up the Ladder from Tot to Tycoon* to the hot breezes of *Footlights and Champagne: I Loved it All.*

I am referring to the decline of serious autobiography, autobiography as the form developed from the Renaissance to World War One: controlled retrospect, the recollected interaction of the *me* and the *not-me* deliberately shaped as a work of literature. A few such autobiographies have been written but none, so far as I know, of sufficient distinction to represent the substantial continuation of the great autobiographical tradition.

Instead, the autobiographic impulse has embodied itself in memoirs (recollection of the times), reminiscences (recollection of friends and family), collected opinions like Maugham's *The Summing-up*, and plain *res gestae*, chronicles of the events of a life. Sir Osbert Sitwell's highly polished volumes well represent the movement of autobiography outward to reminiscence-memoirs; as has been observed, this admirable work "tells us little about what it feels like to be in Sir Osbert's skin." The twentieth century is not the place to seek autobiography in the grand style, such as the *Commentaries* of Aeneas Sylvius Piccolomini.

The decline of the life-relationship as generating force of biography is equally marked. There are notable exceptions, like Ernest Jones' *Life* of Sigmund Freud, but the best modern American and British biographies have sprung from research, not from recollection. Life-relationship biography has, in general, now fallen to the vehicle by which the subordinates of famous military commanders express their admirations (*The Unknown Eisenhower; A Tentmate Looks at Monty*), and the friends of literary giants their frustrations, engendered by the great man—witness in the latter case the sad circle of works enclosing D. H. Lawrence, from Middleton Murry's *Son of Woman* to Richard Aldington's *Portrait of a Genius, But. . . .*

The link between the decline of formal autobiography and the decline of biography sprung from life-relationship—that tradition which until our day produced the world's greatest biographies—can be partly descried, it seems clear, in the force which science, particularly psychology, has exerted upon life-writing. Today the self is more exposed and yet more elusive, more comprehensible but less manageable, more fascinating but not so palatable. Undertaking an autobiography, under the aegis of modern psychology, is like signing a contract with the Devil: there is much to be won and everything, especially honor, to be lost. In the Age of Freud, to look no deeper than Gibbon looked in the Age of Hume is to perpetrate an anachronism; but to subject oneself to even amateur psychological scrutiny seems rather like performing an act of private therapy in public. Hence the autobiographer, skirting the sinister deeps of his personality, roams outward into the happier champaign of memoir-reminiscence.

For the writer contemplating the biography of a friend, as well as for the autobiographer, the fallibility of retrospect has been cruelly revealed; it is impossible to dodge the realization that memory recreates rather than regurgitates the past. Errors of fact may be checked against the record; but the complex of intimate feeling and fond recall, that dome of many-colored glass fragmenting the light of truth—to try to ignore or tinker with that is to confound the impulse willing the biography into existence. We have lost much in losing the brilliant images of memory, the living perception, the flashes of insight springing from intimacy; but, perhaps wisely, we have put our faith in the detachment which accompanies knowledge gained through research. The groper-from-without has fewer traps to fear than the borer-from-within. More practically, in this epoch of paper, a man accumulates so many documentary remains—again the force of science —that a coeval can hardly hope to live long enough to digest them into a biography.

In the second characteristic of modern life-writing, the wide range of biographical activity, we can see most clearly the partial fulfillment of Nicolson's prophecy, the split between the "literary element" and the "scientific element."
Stretched along a rough scale from the most literary-least factual to the most "scientific"-least literary, modern biographies display an infinity of gradations. These resolve themselves, broadly, into some eight perceptible types.
On the radical left appears the novel-as-biography, almost wholly imaginary. Then come the extensive and often marshy reaches of fictionized biography, which stretch from outright romancing to more or less serious biographical intentions. This popular form merges into the more carefully controlled and sometimes remarkably able genre, interpretative biogra-

phy, running to the center of the scale. The Lives on the other side, all of them true to the biographic oath, range from the chief exemplars of modern life-writing, with the best scholarly biographies on the right flank, through the increasingly dense "research" biography, the "life-and-times" biography, what I venture to call the "Behemoth biography," and so to works of such high specific gravity that they are little more than compilations of source-materials. Hovering above the center of the scale appears the radiant-plumaged "super-biography," which seeks to be both ultimately literary and ulmimately scientific.

To the force of literature, the "literary element," the art of life-writing is indebted for that twentieth-century phenomenon, the novel-as-biography—not the novel in the form of a life, *David Copperfield*, but the novel in the form of life-writing. Such works do not, like fictionized biography, masquerade as Lives; rather, they imaginatively take the place of biography where there can be no genuine biography for lack of materials. We have, in the autobiographical form, those brilliant re-creations of Robert Graves, *I, Claudius* and *Claudius the God*, and Mary Renault's *The King Must Die;* in the form of biography, Graves' *Count Belisarius* and Hope Muntz' study of Harold Godwinson, *The Golden Warrior.*

In fictionized biography the seductive influence of the "literary element" is all too apparent. Just as the compiler of biographical information risks no involvement, the fictionizer admits no limit to it. The heady airs of novelistic freedom encourage him to invent, transpose, as he will. The result is usually a flaccid compound of fact and fancy, ill-mated, a sort of mutant.

Interpretative biography, on the other hand, shows now the force of science, as in the "psychological biography" where pseudo-Freudianism cavorts or serious analytical speculation holds sway, and now the force of literature, as in the works which draw on invention to flesh out a scene or to dramatize the substance of a letter by arranging it as conversation or to read the subject's mind. At its responsible best, as in Catherine Drinker Bowen's *Yankee from Olympus*, interpretative biography has produced books of unquestioned worth —though Mrs. Bowen has probably done her finest work since eschewing "interpretation," as in her biography of Coke, *The Lion and the Throne.*

Interpretative biographers in our time have vigorously affirmed that theirs is the true biography and all else, factmongering. Hesketh Pearson jauntily defended interpretative biography on the grounds that since art can do better than fact, it must not be restrained by fact. "No artist worth his salt," he wrote, "is concerned with accuracy of detail if it doesn't happen to suit his purpose. By mere process of selection, he is forced to distort the facts as they would come from the pen of a reporter." But a painter catching on canvas a landscape and a biographer catching on paper a character are artists working from quite different premises. The painter signs a compact with himself to render not the landscape but his vision as honestly as he can; the biographer signs a compact with himself to render his man as honestly as he can. What Pearson called "the mere process of selection" does not necessarily "distort the facts" if it is artfully accomplished; its purpose is to reveal their inner meaning. Even if some distortion occurs, it belongs to another world from deliberate falsification.

Pearson wrote further, "When conversation is used to reveal character, it should be more characteristic of the speaker than his actual everyday conversation. Very often too . . . an imagined anecodote reveals a personality more clearly than a real anecdote." But how can an imitation of a thing be truer to a thing than the thing itself? The biographer does not lumber his pages with "actual everyday conversation," even where such is on record. He selects those moments of conversation, those observations and turns of speech which, he conceives, best characterize his subject. And an "imagined anecdote" can no more provide a genuine revelation than a forged cheque can be used for genuine money. Invented conversations and anecdotes, lacking truth, lack everything.

Pearson pressed his point to the pitch of confusion when he declared that of two quite different character sketches of the same person, the truer is "obviously not the one that contains the greater number of incontrovertible facts, but the one that paints the more living picture." However, it would seem rather obvious that the best character sketch is one in which incontrovertible facts are transmuted into a living picture. The implied comparison with the art of painting trails a red herring. The face of Christ painted by Leonardo may well be a greater work of art than the face of Henry VIII painted by Holbein, but it is not a greater likeness, it is not a likeness at all. The biographer's object is not to create a living picture, but to create a living picture from the materials at hand, to create a living picture which will be a true likeness.

Here and there the practitioner of interpretative biography

has mounted a more fundamental attack. How can it be proved, he demands, that his *invention* of a subject's inner life is not closer to truth than the biographer's *suggestion* of it? Like Pilate, he asks with some scorn, What is Truth? Has the subject told nothing but truth in his letters? Have his friends offered nothing but the truth about his character? Where is truth in a scene reported in contradiction and confusion by three eye-witnesses? Why talk of truth, then, when the materials themselves cannot possibly be entirely accurate, true, reliable? Furthermore, the interpretative biographer affirms, there are the manipulations performed by the biographer himself. He must choose, emphasize, draw conclusions from inconclusive evidence, issue judgments at every turn. What then becomes of truth when materials not true to begin with are exploited by fallible human intelligence? The inner life which is invented, the interpreter concludes, can reveal a truth superior to the so-called truth of facts.

The biographer can only answer that biographical truth is not and can never be absolute truth. He knows too well the fallibility of himself and his materials, and what he engages to tell is the best truth he can find, to the best of his ability. Eschewing unlikely witnesses and unconvincing report, he will indeed make judgments, use his insight and his imagination, but only so far as his pursuit of the real man and the limits of his sources allow. The result may be maimed truth, but the genuine biographer believes that maimed truth is better than, is a world removed from, outright invention.

Toward the right end of the biographical spectrum, where the force of science (but not psychological science) grows ever more insistent, there occurs that loosely named gradation of works, the scholarly biography, the life-and-times biography, the research biography. At its best, this amorphous class of lives has given us, in the multi-volumed *Life of Marlborough* by Winston Churchill and *R. E. Lee* by Douglas Southall Freeman, two of the most accomplished biographies of the age, Lives which deploy a tremendous weight of materials and reveal their subjects in multifarious detail but are so imaginatively powered and so artfully developed that they unfold with sinewy felicity despite enormous bulk—literary grace maintained despite the pressure of facts.

The denser works of this class, those increasingly obedient to fact, I have called "Behemoth biography," not so much for their size but for their mass. The Behemoth biography is not entirely a twentieth-century phenomenon. Masson's *Milton* and Spedding's *Bacon*, and, in the United States, John G. Nicolay and John Hay's *Abraham Lincoln, A History*, in ten volumes, reveal the force of science beginning to press on biography in the nineteenth century. But the modern Behemoth biography represents an intensification of research, a self-conscious dedication to accumulation, a pack-rat expertise, unknown to the Victorians. In the way of insight, of imaginative liaison, the Behemoth biography risks very little and therefore risks a great deal.

Some of these gargantuan Lives are skillfully put together and deserve at least to be called works of enlightened research, but the term *biography* needs some stretching to include them. There is now in hand an extended Life of Ruskin, in the first volume of which John Ruskin just manages to be conceived. In manuscript, Leslie Marchand's *Life* of Byron, it is said, ran to a million words; when cut in half for publication, the work contained some 1200 pages of text and 300 pages of notes. It may be that Byron has sufficient vitality to keep his head above this high tide of fact and discussion. Frank Freidel is locked in an heroic struggle with the two dozen tons of paper that hold the raw materials of Freidel's continuing biography of Franklin Delano Roosevelt. N. I. White's *Shelley*, C. Read's *Francis Walsingham*—all these works, wrought with great care, offer an important service in opening up the intricate reaches of their subjects' lives, but should perhaps be named biographical scholarship rather than biography.

The more egregious Behemoth biographies, however, bury the delicate patterns of human growth and change under the silt of the day-to-day record. Every dredged-up detail must be included. Hence these works, even when literate, lack the shaping pressure of selectivity and the dramatic focus of viewpoint. To accumulate all is to understand all—this bastardization of the scientific attitude rules their roost.

Like the novel-as-biography and the Behemoth biography, that aureate bird soaring above the center of the biographical scale, the superbiography, is a twentieth-century biographical phenomenon. I have used the name *superbiography* because this genre grandly exploits both the "literary element" and the "scientific element" (psychology), yet uses no outright invention and thus presents itself as the ultimate exemplar of modern life-writing. The writer claims to transcend his medium without abandoning it, to disport himself under the Mediterranean sun and yet maintain his primitive Barbarian virtue.

Superbiography is eminently represented today by the

work of Leon Edel, who has produced three volumes of a biography of Henry James which is not yet concluded. In lectures and articles and in a volume, *Literary Biography*, he has also sought to revive "the great and lively discussion" about biography of the 1920's in order to "bring biography into mid-century focus." In these critical writings, Edel has, in effect, produced a defense of the methods which he uses in his biography of Henry James.

He contends that the biographer can remain faithful to truth and yet move with the freedom of the artist, that is, that he can employ the methods and assume the omniscience of the novelist. "The biographer," he declares, "may be as imaginative as he pleases—the more imaginative the better—in the way in which he brings together his materials, but he must not imagine the materials." With Lytton Strachey as his inspiration, Strachey representing the triumph of the artist over the accumulator, Edel develops the conception, in his *Literary Biography*, that the materials of biography can bear any amount of fragmentation, that the superbiographer is a sort of novelist of truth—"He may shuttle backward and forward in a given life; he may seek to disengage scenes or utilize trivial incidents . . . to illuminate character; he has so saturated himself with his documents that he may cut himself free from their bondage without cutting himself free from their truth."

It is all very seductive. The trouble is, materials of biography are not infinitely plastic. They are not the same kind of materials as the materials of the novelist, and the same kind of methods cannot be applied to them indiscriminately. Omniscience, which is an essential function of the novelist, becomes a distracting intrusion of the biographer. Just as a rearrangement of atoms will produce an alteration of substance, so a fragmentation of biographical materials, to secure a free manipulation of their elements, ruptures the patterns of life. When the biographer apes the novelist, he loses the sense of life being lived by the subject and produces, as a substitute, the life being lived, as it were, by the biographer. We take it for granted that the novelist must be the lord of his material; as master conjurer, he creates a world in which, if he is a good novelist, we will believe. We expect the biographer, however, not to *refashion* but to *elicit* the shapes and meanings within his material; and if he acts as conjurer, he does not call into being a world but interposes his prestidigitation between us and the world.

As long ago as 1790, a biographer named Edward Topham saw this: "We must follow nature. All acted character [that is, artificial manipulation of character] is a miserable thing; and the extravagant relation of it is less interesting still than the thing itself." The "extravagant relation" of the novelist creates out of invented materials the illusion of life; the same "extravagant relation," applied to the materials of biography, destroys that illusion. Instead of being persuaded to live the life along with the subject, we are never permitted to forget that we are living that life under the aegis of the biographer.

In his *Aspects of Biography*, André Maurois points out that, "It is always a mistake, in a biography, to anticipate. 'This great statesman was born in a small village . . .' No baby is a great statesman. Every man discovers successively the ages and aspects of life." But, cries Mr. Edel, "When I pick up a biography, I know before I open the book that it is the life of a statesman. . . . Our point of departure in the reading of a biography is not necessarily in the cradle, but with the man who achieved greatness . . ." Maurois, Edel comments, "wants us to play a rather curious game of make-believe."

But this is precisely what we do when we read biography. Just as in other arts we are willing to suspend our disbelief, so in reading biography, we are willing to suspend our knowledge. We do not insist on remembering that Napoleon won the battle of Austerlitz when we read about his childhood. On the contrary, when we enter upon the life of a great man, we put aside what we happen to know about him, and if the biographer is skillful at his business, we are willing, indeed we are anxious, to begin with the child and live a life along with him into greatness. Maurois is quite right: no statesman or athletes or warriors are born—only babies. If Edel insists on reminding us what our subject is *going to be,* how can we possibly lose ourselves in any moment when he *is?*

It is this question of time which particularly interests him; it is the free manipulation of time by the novelist which he particularly claims for the biographer.

Edel declares, "I see no reason why biographers should not move easily through time, and anticipate and tell the story in the very best way they can, forward and backward. . . . By doing this . . . we make a person seem more alive, less an individual living his life solely by the calendar and the clock." In sum, "Biography can violate chronology without doing violence to truth."

There are two rather obvious answers to this argument. In the first place, a novel usually pictures only a segment of a life—a few years or months or even weeks. The novelist shuttles forward and backward in time in order to enrich that segment, to offer glimpses of the growth of character, to sketch in the past out of which the present has developed, in short, to suggest by fracturing time, the large unfolding of life that occurs in the real world. But the biographer begins with what the novelist must seek to suggest: his misson *is* the unfolding of an entire life as it occurred in the real world. Thus, if the biographer manipulates time like the novelist, he is, in effect, seeking to secure what he already has, and what, ironically enough, he may in thus seeking lose. It is not so much gilding as gelding the lily. What the novelist does with time to make an imaginary person seem real may very well tend to make a real person seem imaginary. Put a creature of human time in novelistic time and he is likely to take on novelistic coloring.

In the second place, the manipulation of time, regardless of its novelistic associations, ruptures the essential dimension of life. When Edel talks scornfully of mechanical time he confuses the measuring instrument with the thing measured. The clock is simply a convenience. Human time means organic change—the grand pattern of growth, maturation, and decay. To abuse that pattern is to abuse the life itself. Human time also means sequential experience, a cumulative process of interaction of the "me" and the "not-me"—of man and the world—creating the continual *becoming* of human character which ends only in death.

Now, it is obvious that the sequential experience of real life cannot be sedulously imitated by the biographer; and Edel is quite right to point out in his *Literary Biography* the leaden flatness of day-to-day biographical chronicling, which is an uninspired way out of the dilemma. The best biographers seek to *suggest* the intricate flow of sequential experience, the simultaneous unfolding of many life-patterns, even as they are forced, by the imperious demand of clarity, to follow one strand after another, to group their materials.

Edel makes much of grouping, as though the technique were the discovery of the superbiographer, but it is, of course, to be found everywhere in the long world-stream of life-writing from Suetonius and Einhard to the present. What matters, today, is that grouping must always be subdued to the large becoming of a life, that it must not be permitted to harden into topical analyses suggesting the on-marching sub-heads of an expository essay, and that the grouping must not do violence to the particular moment which is chosen as the nucleus for thematic clustering.

Oddly enough, the example of grouping in his *James* which Edel chooses to discuss in *Literary Biography* commits just this violence. The nucleus is a visit James paid to Emerson in 1870, and the passage, abridged, runs as follows:

> Emerson's notebooks show no record of the visit: but then young Henry James came to him in all familiarity. . . . The nearby woods were showing their autumn colors; an aroma of apples hung over the sleepy town. . . . Henry saw his father's friend in his well-known and homely surroundings. . . . Hawthorne was but six years dead; Thoreau eight. It was as if they still lived, as if the great moment in the town's history had not yet passed—that moment when there resided at one end of Concord a sage whose utterances were "the most poetical, the most beautiful productions of the American mind" while at the other—with rows of tall New England elms between—there lived an

exquisite teller of tales.

Again and again Henry was to use the word "exquisite" in speaking of Emerson and Hawthorne. . . . He was to wander later with Emerson in the Louvre and the Vatican. "But his spirit, his moral taste, as it were, abode always within the undecorated walls of his youth." So, too, Henry remarked, Hawthorne had spent fifty years in small American towns. . . . He too had been "exquisitely and consistently provincial."

The meeting of Emerson and the young writer in that early autumn was a meeting of past and future. Henry always remembered Emerson's voice: it was "irresistible" and he had a "beautiful mild modest authority." He also had (and Henry was to remark on this again and again) "that ripe unconsciousness of evil which is one of the most beautiful signs by which we know him." The Emersonian innocence, the exquisite provinciality of it, touched Henry deeply. . . . However, it gave the future novelist food for thought—that Emerson had considered Hawthorne's novels "not worthy of him." . . . Emerson's insensibility to imaginative writers, from Shelley to Dickens, Dante to Jane Austen, Aristophanes to Cervantes—Henry enumerated them— was "a large allowance to have to make for a man of letters."

Edel makes much of the fact that he did not use the materials of this passage in chronological order, that is, noting for the year 1870 the visit to Concord, then chronicling in due sequence the meetings in Europe two years later, James' attending Emerson's funeral in 1883, and James writing an article on Emerson in 1887:

> In my mind all this material melts together into a portrait of the two, the young man and the old, the one at the beginning of his career, the other near the end, in Concord, at the Louvre, at the Vatican. I can place my scene in Concord in

1870—for this is where Emerson belonged and where both can best be placed in their American setting. . . . In creating this scene I violate no fact. I put no thoughts into James's head or into Emerson's. I adhere to the one point of view in my possession, James', and try to set down his vision and perception—which he recorded—of the man of Concord. But from Concord I leap into the future, to Europe and back again, and to the funeral, and to Concord again as Henry James viewed it when he himself was old. . . .

I do this in violation of all chronology, dealing with my subject's relation to Emerson at the most meaningful moment that I can find. . . . By weaving backward and forward in time and even dipping into the future . . . I reckon with time, as it really exists, as something fluid and irregular and with memory as something alive and flickering and evanescent. I refuse to be fettered by the clock and the calendar. I neither depart from my documents nor do I disparage them. . . . If I paint carefully, and do my utmost not to falsify the colors, there is no reason why I should not in the end be able to hang before my reader a reasonable likeness . . . instead of offering him a card index, a cluttered worktable, or a figure of papier-mâché.

Since Edel makes so much of this grouping, we may take it, I suppose, as a show-piece of his claim to assume the omniscience of the novelist, to rupture sequential experience at his will, to "be as imaginative as he pleases . . . in the way in which he brings together his materials," and yet to remain true to them and to the biographer's oath.

The passage, no doubt of it, is brilliantly ingenious. But it violates truth from beginning to end. Not the truth of words, which is child's truth, but the truth of mind-and-time, which is biographical truth.

In the first place, in bleeding his documents of their time-significance, he cuts them loose, wan entities, from the truth of an unfolding life. To hang upon the hook of the 1870 visit what James thought of Emerson in 1887, to declare that truth is preserved when the recorded opinion of a middle-aged man is transferred to the youthful mind of that man, rests on the curiously naive assumption, apparently, that human growth and change can be bypassed without injury to actuality.

As a rounding up of what Henry James, in sum, felt about Emerson, the passage cannot be faulted . . . cannot be faulted, that is, as exposition cunningly veneered with scenic effects. As a picture of what young Henry was thinking of Emerson in 1870, it is exactly that which Edel denies stooping to, invention. For example, Edel has no way of knowing that during the 1870 visit Emerson's denigration of Hawthorne's fiction was giving "the future novelist food for thought." It was the established novelist who was made uneasy by that judgment.

"By weaving backward and forward in time," Edel emphasizes, "and even dipping into the future [as Henry himself could not dip] . . . I reckon with time as it really exists [but not for Henry], as something fluid and irregular and with memory as something alive and flickering and evanescent [whose memory?]."

As applied to the Emerson grouping, this observation— as I have tried to suggest by my interjections—serves to underline that the passage offers only a masquerade of "a reasonable likeness."

Young James, in 1870, could hardly *remember* what he was to think of Emerson in 1887. The "memory" which is recreated as "something alive and flickering" is not James' at all. It is Edel's "synthetic" memory; it is the author imposing on the subject *his* view of the whole James-Emerson relationship. The "time, as it really exists" is Edel's time, not James'. Thus is exposed the fallibility of the omniscient viewpoint applied to life-writing. It is the superbiographer's consciousness, the superbiographer's time, which dominate and order, not the subject's time. It is Edel who stands in the center of things, not James. Three-quarters of a century ago James Parton pointed out how a biographer should treat his subject—"Let *him* have the whole floor."

Now if Edel had used James' presence at Emerson's funeral, for example, as the nucleus for his grouping, then he might well have been able to suggest the play of James' mind backward and forward, among his childhood memory, his 1870 visit, and his view of Emerson in 1883. As it is, he does not "adhere to the one point of view in my possession, James'," but rather substitutes his own point of view, an invented retrospect. To seek imaginatively to get inside the skin of the subject is admirable, but Edel here goes so far, in effect, as to write a segment of James' autobiography, as James might have composed it had he enjoyed Edel's understanding of himself.

Finally, this artful legerdemain actually falsifies what appears to have been Henry James' view of Emerson, *at that time*, and, as well, ignores the opportunity of juxtaposing it with Emerson's response to the visit. Two pages before Edel embarks on his grouping, he notes, without comment, that James wrote of his visit, "I spent lately a couple of days with Mr. Emerson at Concord—pleasantly, *but with slender profit* [my italics]." This cool observation, by the young cosmopolitan, is rather different from the mellow admiration of 1887 which is thrust into its place. At the conclusion of the grouping Edel notes, again without comment, that Emerson, "a day or two after Henry's visit," wrote to Carlyle, "A multitude of young men are growing up here of high promise, and I compare gladly the social poverty of my youth with the power on which these draw."

Played against the *summary* of James' view of Emerson, as it is, this statement is deprived of the poignantly ironical meaning it suggests when placed in contrast with young Henry's offhand comment. Edel's reconstruction fails both by omission and commission. In concluding that the only alternative to the superdistortions of superbiography is "a card index, a cluttered worktable," Edel chooses to ignore, or is unaware of, the best biographical writing of his age.

Shift a human being around arbitrarily in time and the delicate web of simulation woven by the biographer is ineluctably broken. The biographer must be the servant, and the subject, the master, of the life being simulated. When the biographer wrenches awry the fundamental dimension of existence to impose an arbitrary time scheme, he becomes the master, and the subject, the servant. In trying to be more of an artist, he becomes less of a biographer.

Edel's first volume of his life of Henry James, *The Untried Years*, illustrates what happens when the biographer moves freely in time. Between the birth of Henry James and Henry's arrival at the age of three, Edel produces a violent and intricate time manipulation: he whisks us to Henry's fourteenth year, in Paris, then to later recollections of Paris which he associates with a scene in *The Ambassadors*, then to a night-

mare, which James recorded in old age; the nightmare is ana-
lyzed at length, particularly for what it reveals about Henry's
relations with his brother; further psychological speculation
ensues concerning James' Parisian experience followed by a
shift to Henry living in Paris at the age of seventeen; and
finally, after additional manipulations of Henry's early mem-
ories, we come to the three-year-old boy dwelling in Albany,
New York.

It is all enormously skillful, psychologically pyrotechnic,
artfully projected. But is it biography? Where is the cumulative unfolding of the child's life? If a reader exclaims in closing the volume, "What an ingenious biography!" the end of
biography is defeated. When he says, "What a fascinating
life," the biographer has achieved his purpose. Instead of simu-
lating a life, Edel sometimes takes us on a conducted tour of
Henry James' nervous system. We do not live James' life
along with James; for we are so bemused by the dexterity of
the clinician that we can hardly discern the predicament of the
patient.

Edel's reaction against life-writing dominated by fact has
likewise carried him into realms inimicable to life-writing
itself.

Into overt psychoanalysis, for one thing. Instead of using
the insights psychology can offer, he deploys the machinery of
psychoanalysis on the page. Biography, however, demands
synthesis, not analysis; the life being lived, not the speculative
chatter of the biographer. "But," demands Edel, "why should
a psychological speculation, based on carefully gathered
data . . . not be as valid as pages of endless and inconclusive
speculation about the first night of *Twelfth Night* . . . ?"

The answer is that neither sort of speculation is valid for biography.

Edel's attitude in his biographical criticism, as well as in the *James*, reveals the intoxicating effects of that heady brew, Literary Significance mixed with Psychological Mastery. To authors not so Olympian as James, and James' biographer, he can be elaborately condescending, as when, in *Literary Biography*, he dismisses Hervey Allen's careful docketing of his records with the remark, "Often it is the lesser scribbler who accumulates the most papers . . ." Nor does he hesitate to inform us that in examining James' letters, "I have found it possible to sort out the exact meaning of his relationship with his correspondents." The *exact* meaning? One doubts that Henry James himself sorted that out.

Edel likewise finds nothing paradoxical in the fact that, whereas he relegates Behemoth biographies to the rank of "source books, from which the other biographers write the readable single-volume lives," he himself, with three volumes of his Henry James already behind him, is preparing to give us at least a fourth. Apparently there are elephants—and elephants.

Compare Edel's attitude with the conclusion of a lecture in which Mark Schorer discusses the writing of his distinguished biography of Sinclair Lewis: "I am not a better man, certainly, for having written his life; but I think that I am a wiser one. And I can only hope that my gratitude to him for that will lighten a little the onus of the life with which I have burdened him."

For all his great talents, Edel unfortunately lacks a cardinal biographical virtue. While life-writing begins in hope, it must end in humility. It is only the other one who counts, the subject.

Ironically enough, the intrusive analyses, the groupings by synthetic retrospect, the arbitrary detachment of materials from their time-context, smother the sense of a life being lived just as surely as do the "card indexes" of the Behemoth biographer whom Edel despises.

His work vividly reveals the vaulting ambitions, and the glittering attainments, of superbiography, as it too exuberantly lays hand on all that literature and psychology have to offer, as it seeks to melt (a favorite Edel word) the psychologist and the novelist into one superbiographer. Quite literally, it is too good to be true. Edel's assimilation of Henry James, despite its modernity, exudes a feral whiff of cannibalism; one almost feels transported to a primitive society in which a spring rite of love ends in consumption instead of consummation.

Edel not only plays the omniscient author, a role he is well suited to, but also the omnipresent author. He is capable of great things, but staying out of the picture is not one of them. The seduction of the "literary element" most obviously shows itself in his determination not only to use all the going devices of the novelist but to use them in full view of the audience; just as the scientific element can be most easily seen in his insistence upon interrupting, or reordering, the texture of James' life in order to display his powers of analysis (which, however, are very impressive). The pretensions of omniscience, in the literary *and* the scientific sense, here conjoin. The resultant spectacle is certainly art, but is it biographical art? An admirer of Edel's may reply, with some justice, that if it is art, nothing else matters. On the other hand, it is perhaps of some moment that in consequence of Edel's superbiography we are not likely to have a biography of James for some time to come; and it is of great moment that superbiography may draw in its wake talents that will be lost to genuine life-writing.

Superbiography represents the most assertive practice of modern biography—practice carried to an extreme which goes beyond the biographical frame and which, therefore, if widely imitated, augurs a decline of the art of life-writing into self-conscious expertise and Corinthian sophistication.

Finally, we come to the third characteristic of modern life-writing, a biographical practice established in the twentieth century which produces in Great Britain and the United States what I take to be the best biographies of our time. Outwardly, except for their accomplishment, they are not so clearly grouped as the superbiographies, the Behemoth biographies, even the interpretative biographies. Yet, at least in those I have studied and those that I have some knowledge of, there can be perceived something like a common approach to the problems of biographical composition, a framework of endeavor, a developing tradition of life-writing which distinctly reveals a specialized interaction of the sensibilities and forces of our age.

Diverse though they are in style, temperament, techniques, such British Lives as Churchill's *Marlborough*, C. V. Wedgwood's *Strafford*, Lord David Cecil's *Melbourne*, R. Hart-Davis' *Hugh Walpole*, Sir John Neale's *Queen Elizabeth*, Harold Nicolson's *George V.*, and such American works as Mark Schorer's *Sinclair Lewis*, Andrew Turnbull's *Scott*

Fitzgerald, C. D. Bowen's *The Lion and the Throne*, S. E. Morison's life of Columbus, *Admiral of the Ocean Sea*, Garrett Mattingly's *Catherine of Aragon*, James L. Clifford's *Young Sam Johnson*, Freeman's *Lee*, Herschel Baker's *William Hazlitt* have all been shaped by a similar awareness of biographical opportunities, a similar perception of literary and scientific possibilities, a sense of the position of the biographer in the biography which was unknown to the past as a practicing principle.

For this kind of biography I can find no convenient term; it represents a double conjunction of science and literature and includes a variety of talents. What happens in the making of such works is what provides the decisive test of the grouping: A simulation of a life, in words, springs from a simulated life-relationship.

I have suggested earlier that, though the cross-tides of science and literature have exerted a disruptive force on life-writing, there has likewise occurred in recent years a beneficent drawing together of the "literary element" and the "scientific element." This drawing-together goes deeper than the present-day scholar's ambition to achieve literary grace and the writer's willingness to forgo "interpretation" and nourish his insight on rigorous research.

The simulation of a life attained by our best biographers grows from the conjuction of heightened perception, the dowry of psychology, and the realization of that perception in the literary projection of experience, the dramatic unfolding of personality-in-action. But the spiritual operation, if I may call it so, which makes heightened perception possible, even more essentially characterizes this mode of modern life-

writing. The simulation of the life grows out of a liaison with
the subject self-consciously cultivated by the biographer as
the *primum mobile* of his enterprise. This liaison I have awk-
wardly named a simulated life-relationship.

The mode of double-simulation begins in detachment, a
fortuitous detachment, a detachment the writer has struggled
neither for nor against but which, as the fundamental condition of his calling, he must confront. He, a living being, faces a
mass of paper, the dreadfully inert remains of his subject—as
all biographers have done. But as never before, the present-
day biographer is conscious of this disparate and incongruous
pairing, himself and paper, and also of what must be done
about it. Brooding over the materials warms them into being,
transforms them from subject matter to the subject himself, a
fellow-being, to whom the biographer becomes, in one way
or another, deeply, vitally attached.

The impartiality of the referee belongs to the world of
sport, not to biography. As Francis Bacon remarked to a
friend (cited by Mrs. Bowen in her *Life* of Bacon), "I will
not question whether you . . . pass for a disinterested man
or no; I freely confess myself am not and so I leave it." Impartiality, indeed, consists in the absence, or feigned absence of
feeling, whereas the biographer, the particular kind of biographer I am talking about, must work from feeling, and all the
subliminal tides that "feeling" connotes. Feeling brought
under control, feeling-become-will, feeling refined by purpose.

Once this living bond is developed between man alive and
man dead, what Mark Schorer finely calls this "symbiotic relationship"—inevitable for all biographers but today con-

sciously nurtured and directed—it is then transmuted into the relationship of artist and subject.

Schorer has briefly revealed the process at work as he undertook the life of Sinclair Lewis: "I began to wonder about my relationship to Sinclair Lewis . . . and . . . to understand how much of that relationship was making the substance of the book." What the writer has submitted to as a human being he must now dominate as a biographer. He has accepted commitment in order to struggle for detachment, this time a willed detachment, one with the seeds of biography swelling within it, a detachment similar to that which he would have to seek if he had known the subject in life. Feeling must be translated into understanding, involvement into insight. The battle is waged to win, not a cold objectivity—the biographer is no unmoved god peering through a microscope—but the kind of love that finds no contradiction between *engagement* and truth.

Out of this nettle, the danger of a bond like that developed in life, the biographer seeks to pluck the flower of perception. A life-relationship has been simulated in order to achieve the simulation of a life.

It is this primary psychological struggle, as well as the psychological-literary struggle for realization, which makes the creation of a biography in this modern mode so arduous a mission. It is not only the research, it is not only the composition, it is also the establishment of a life-giving "symbiotic relationship"—this in-between, dark, silent wrestling—which stretches out the years of the germination of biography.

A secret wrestling—yet one of its manifestations can be readily discerned.

This modern biographer is acutely conscious of the importance of *locale*. The settings in which the subject passed his
life, his houses and his clothes and his furniture, the battle-
fields he fought over, the woods in which he walked, his quill
pen and his manuscripts, the theatrical boards he trod, the
village lane invisibly marked by his scuffing boyhood, the
vistas of town and country on which he fed his heart—from
these enduring ambiences, atmospheric and substantial, the
biographer elicits both aid and comfort, information and,
name never to be named, inspiration.

Most obviously, by studying the subject's habitat, the
places most decisively associated with his experience, the biographer secures all kinds of "background material" enabling
him to enrich his work in many ways—develop a scene in
detail, follow accurately his subject's movement from room to
room, unroll the panorama of a battlefield, picture the street
down which the subject walked one rainy morning, to triumph or to doom.

Likewise, these physical ambiences sometimes enable the life-
writer to tighten his grip on character, even to solve enigmas
of behavior, mysterious responses to experience. In working
on a life of Richard III, for example, I felt that in immersing
myself in the wild reaches of the Yorkshire dales which Richard passionately loved, I was able to see more clearly into his
alienation from the proto-Renaissance court of his brother,
Edward IV. That which a man loves—a house, a stream, a
hat—can sometimes express him as clearly as what he says and
does.

This complex, subtle, frequently inarticulate relationship
between biographer and locale affects not only the simula-

tion of the life but also the simulation of the life-relationship. The interaction of biographer and subject is heightened by the biographer's direct, sensory experience of the matrix from which the subject's experience has been shaped. The biographer opens himself to all that places and things will tell him, in his struggle to visualize, and to sense, his man in being.

Deepest of all, the particular kind of biographer of whom I am speaking, cherishes, I believe, a conviction—call it a romantic quirk, if you will—that where the subject has trod he must tread, what the subject has seen he must see, because he thus achieves an indefinable but unmistakable kinship with his man. The winning of this kinship, more than anything else he can do, helps to annihilate the centuries, the spaces, the deceptions of change, the opacity of death.

Even those who, like myself, but labor to approach this mode of composition, without any illusions of having mastered it, are moved by this power of place. It would be vain for me to assert that the biography of Louis XI on which I am working will be demonstrably abler because I have held in my hand—within the whispering vault of Cléry, the church he built—the massive skull which still, by the language of sheer bone, bespeaks the marvelously ugly countenance of that consummate actor. Yet, in many excursions across the Field of Montlhéry, "the field of tears," where Louis fought, under circumstances which dramatically reveal the motions of his character, a wild, bloody battle with his mortal foe, Charles of Burgundy, I believe that I learned more than the physical appearance of the terrain and the probable movements of the armies.

Philippe de Commynes describes the ground as it looked

before the battle—fields of wheat and beans shimmering under a bitter July sun—and then the after-battle scene of dust-clouds hanging in the torrid air, dead men and horses strewn in furrows, the green-and-gold grain now smashed into the earth.

On just such a July day I first climbed the ridge of Montlhéry to gaze at the countryside below—and there stood fields of wheat and beans shimmering in the sun, there lay the village canted on the hillside, and at my back, gray stone walls of the royal castle. Perhaps I am deceived in thinking that what then happened to me was more than a *frisson*, a literary thrill. I can but report that I felt a shock of recognition, a poignant apprehension of Louis that I had not previously achieved.

When it comes to the marrow of such a biographical liaison, only one's own testimony can bear witness. I take the liberty of suspecting, however, that Mark Schorer hunting Sinclair Lewis through Italy, Morison furrowing the ocean in the wake of Columbus, Mrs. Bowen pursuing the Rubensteins into Russia and John Adams through his New England haunts, have likewise felt that they derived from their cultivation of enduring ambiences something more than information, even than insight. Like the force of psychology and the native power of understanding, the seeking-out of place operates both on the simulation of the life and the anterior simulation of the life-relationship.

This practice of modern biography, a double simulation conjointly fostered by science and literature, has not produced towering masterpieces nor flamboyant experimentation, nor tigers of the week who stalk through the reviews. It has no Hemingway nor even a D. H. Lawrence, no Eugene O'Neill, no angry young men in Britain or angry young mentors in America. But this dually-simulative mode of composition, growing in accomplishment and in authority, is probably creating the most sustained pitch of biographical excellence that the world has yet enjoyed.

For all the aids and the threats, the buffets, hopes, ill auguries posed by modern civilization, biography remains a coarse tough art inured to vicissitudes and desperately straddling the rainbow and the stone. A craft with a strangely checkered history. A craft of the impossible.

With "gentle Shakespeare" and "deep-browed" Homer and exquisitely nervous Shelley and earth-warm Whitman and visionary Tolstoi and that golden bowl of sensibility, Henry James, and magisterial Eliot and serene Sophocles to create our masterpieces of poetry, novel, drama, is it not the appropriate fate of biography that a James Boswell, the undignified and unedifying Laird of Auchinlech, created the *Life of Johnson*? What is worse, biography is *proud* of Boswell. But then, it is prompted by a bizarre muse. Those who to her hearken live in the dark of the moon and feed on curds and wonder.

Index

DATE DUE

☞			
GAYLORD			PRINTED IN U.S.A.